DEADWOOD
A TALE OF BUNK IN
THE BLACK HILLS

DEADWOOD
A TALE OF BUNK IN
THE BLACK HILLS

By

Len Wildes

ISBN# 1-58721-149-1

1stBooks rev. 5/03/00

About the Book

"Deadwood" is a wild ride through the Old West during the summer of 1876. History may tell you that this was the same summer Will Bill Hickok and General George Custer bit the dust. Don't believe it. Larger-than-life heroes are hard to find so every once in awhile we must recycle them to live and fight another day. These Legends of the West reunite in Deadwood Gulch – a rowdy, bawdy, sleazy, raunchy settlement on the last frontier. Calamity Jane, Buffalo Bill Cody, Crazy Horse, Henry M. Stanley and a cast of colorful characters of the day join them in their misadventures. Although based on alleged events of the times, the novel was written for entertainment values and not redeeming social values. It is a wink in the eye of history. It is a tale of lusty men and their sometimes even lustier women. The reader may even learn a thing or two about the Old West. But it really isn't necessary.

HISTORY SAYS: George Armstrong Custer was killed by Indians on June 26, 1876, on Last Stand Hill, near the Little Big Horn River in Montana.

HISTORY SAYS: James Butler (a.k.a. Wild Bill) Hickok was killed by Jack McCall on August 2, 1876, in No. 10 Saloon, in Deadwood Gulch, in Dakota Territory.

HENRY FORD SAYS: History is bunk.

ONE

James Butler Hickok's face was a death mask. There was no movement, no motion, as his unblinking eyes stared at the five cards gripped tightly in his hands. He was as still and stiff as death. Until...

"I'm a patient man, myself, Bill, but for mercy sake, make weigh or drop anchor," said Captain Massey, a former Missouri River boat pilot and present card crony of the man known far and wide as Wild Bill Hickok, Prince of Pistoleers.

Captain Massey's comment on the painfully deliberative card-playing strategy of Mister Hickok brought chuckles from the two other men at the table; Carl Mann, partner in the No. 10, and Charlie Rich, a pain-in-the-ass on a good day but today a hemorrhoid on a mastodon.

Charlie Rich was sitting in Mister Hickok's seat, the one against the wall, which provided him with a panoramic view of the saloon and its occupants, a valuable nugget of knowledge for a man who lived by the gun but was not particularly enthralled in dying by it.

Mister Hickok glanced over his shoulder and gave a cool look towards the disreputable-looking character that suddenly appeared in the doorway. When he turned his attention back to the card table, the character took a quick step inside.

Once again Mister Hickok asked the grinning Charlie Rich for his regular seat. Once again Charlie Rich grinned.

1

"Damn't, Charlie, give Bill his stool or I'll come over and lay this along side your bony head," declared bartender Harry Young, as he waved a large bung mallet.

He turned and winked at me as I let down my mug of beer and once again began writing in my tablet. Although personally knowing Mister Hickok for six weeks, I was still awed by his presence. He was my hero. I first read about him in the dime and half-dime novels as a boy in Wilkes-Barre and continued reading about him between mining and engineering studies at the small rural college back East where I graduated in June.

Even though I had long since learned that the stories in the novels, as well as in newspapers, were mostly bunk, Mister Hickok exceeded his reputation.

Looking at him now, I thought of the article written by Henry Morton Stanley in the New York Herald a year ago:

"He is thirty-eight years old and is as handsome a specimen of a man as could be found. He held himself straight, and had broad, compact shoulders, was large chested, with small waist and well-formed muscular limbs. A fine handsome face, free from blemish, a light moustache, a thin pointed nose, bluish-gray eyes, with a calm look, magnificent forehead, hair parted from the center of the forehead and hanging down behind the ears in wavy, silken curls, made up the most picturesque figure."

Mister Stanley had a penchant for the purple but this time his description of Mister Hickok's physical appearance was correct. But it was doubtful he could describe the man inside. Even I, who practically walked in his footsteps, had difficulty accepting the contrasts. At all times he was polite and accommodating with all he encountered. But, then, with his reputation, he could afford to be. I still find it hard to believe Mister Hickok had killed thirty-seven. That was more or less the official count and did not include Indians or Confederate soldiers.

I also found it hard to believe that Mister Hickok was allowing Charlie Rich to plague him. No one would dare to do this in the past. If the likes of a Charlie Rich took his chair, or anything else for that matter, he would have departed either head first or feet first.

Mister Hickok's partner, Colorado Charlie Utter, had told me Mister Hickok at thirty-nine years of age was at peace with the world. He had mellowed.

"Charlie, damn't, give Bill his stool or I'll..."

"That's all right, Harry, Charlie was just about to trade chairs. Isn't that right, Charlie?"

"Sure, Bill, of course. Certainly," Charlie Rich said as he jumped up. Even a dullard like him could not mistake the tone in Mister Hickok's voice.

"Sit down. We'll finish the hand first," Mister Hickok said and again stared unblinkingly at his cards.

The disreputable-looking character—even a standout in his cornucopia of disreputable-looking characters—left the doorway and walked carelessly, perhaps too carelessly, to the bar.

He stood next to me. I moved. Not far or fast enough. The smell caught up.

"Put some money on the bar, Jack McCall, or leave," said Harry Young. "This is a public house, not a pest house."

"You'll see my money when I'm good and ready," McCall said and sauntered over to the card table. He stopped at a point a few yards from Mister Hickok. He swiftly drew an old revolver from his waistband and aimed it at the back of Mister Hickok's head.

"Take that, damn you," he shouted.

Before anyone could give a warning, a shot rang out.

McCall was thrust forward. He landed in the middle of the table, his face in the poker pot. Blood pumped from a hole in the back of his head.

Outlined in the doorway by the afternoon sun stood General George Armstrong Custer, a smoking gun in his hand.

"By God, men, it is the coward of the Little Big Horn," declares Carl Mann.

General Custer's eyes narrow. In one smooth motion he cocks the hammer on the large revolver and brings it to bear on Mann.

"That's what they say, those smart-alecky newspapers. They call you that. I always knew you had good reason to leave your command before the Indians attacked. Reno and Benteen are the

3

real cowards, not you." Perspiration flowed like a spring thaw over Mann's now white face. "Please don't shoot me, General. I never said you were a yellow-bellied deserter; a rat jumping ship; a disgrace to your…"

By now General Custer's right eye is ticking violently.

"Shut up Carl before he talks himself into being shot," Harry Young whispers.

I step over and deliver a right jab to Mann's jaw. He collapses in a heap on the sawdust-covered floor.

"Not that way," Harry Young said as he rushed around the bar and grabbed one of Mann's arms, indicating to me to take the other. "But it did the job." The limp body is deposited in an empty chair.

General Custer, unlike the other patrons, did not get a laugh out of this. He kept the big revolver pointing at Mann.

While this was going on, Mister Hickok grabbed the deadman's head by the hair, lifted it off the poker pot and squinted at it. (There were those who said he was losing his eyesight because he sometimes wore blue-tinted eye spectacles. But he said they were just his sun-protection glasses.

"Broken Nose McCall. I never did trust you," Mister Hickok declared and unceremoniously dropped the head back on the table. But away from the poker pot. He wiped the blood from his hand on the deadman's shirt, and in a voice barely audible, "Anybody beat aces and eights?"

A pair of aces and a pair of eights would be a fair hand in draw poker but not something to bet the family farm on in Seven Up, the game being played.

With this out of the way, he turned to General Custer.

"You were always a friend in need, George, I'm just sorry I couldn't have been there in your need." Mister Hickok appeared to wipe a tear from his eye. "I didn't receive your telegram until after I learned of the tragic news. Whatever you want, just ask…"

General Custer nodded. His right eye was still ticking and he was still aiming the big revolver at the now awake but still perspiring and still white Mann.

4

"Move aside son so I can plug a couple of holes in his windjammer."

I suddenly discovered, much to my chagrin, I was the only object between General Custer's line of fire and Carl Mann. Harry Young pantomimed to me not to move. Easy for him; he was behind the bar.

Mann was a decent sort—both he and his partner Jerry Lewis treated me with respect; possibly because of my journalistic prowess, but more than likely because of my association with Mister Hickok. Mann was also a friend of Mister Hickok and supplied him with food and drink as long as he used the No. 10 as his headquarters.

"Now, George, ole pard, you're not going to shoot Carl here, are you? He didn't mean anything. He was just repeating all of this bunk that's going around."

"Bill's right, General. There's just so much bunk going around. Please don't shoot me."

General Custer's eye was now down to a slow tick. But he still had the big revolver pointed at Mann and I was still in the line of fire.

"Hell, George, if you shoot Carl, he won't be able to give us meals and booze on the house. Isn't that right, Carl?"

"Certainly is, Bill. I won't be able to serve the General the best steaks and finest whiskey in the Black Hills. None of that buffalo hide and rotgut we serve everyone else. Nothing but the cream for Wild Bill Hickok and General George Armstrong Custer."

"Well…" General Custer said as he uncocked his revolver.

"Besides," Mister Hickok added, "if you kill every fool who tells that abominable lie, there won't be anyone left to hear the truth. And, by God, George, they are going to hear the truth."

The Legends of the West walked towards each other and embraced.

This had to be an historic moment. General Custer—he was officially a lieutenant colonel, the major general rank was a brevet honor earned during the Civil War—was almost as handsome as Mister Hickok. He shared the fine facial features and hard eyes. His hair and moustache, though much lighter in color, were almost as long as Mister Hickok's. The last time I saw General Custer, two months ago, his hair had been cut short for the campaign.

I consulted another tablet in my pocket. Let's see, if Mister Hickok is thirty-nine, then General Custer is thirty-six.

Carl Mann and Jerry Lewis lifted the corpse off the table and "walked" it towards the door.

"What should we do with him?" asked Mann.

"Shove a bone up his ass and let the dogs drag him through the streets," suggested Harry Young.

"We'll prop him next to the door outside and get Doc Peirce to bury him," Lewis said.

"When you get Doc, tell him to look at my arm," said Captain Massey, who was holding his left arm. "The General's bullet went clear through that son-of-a-bitch's head."

"Get him over here," said Harry Young as he leaned over the bar. "Get your coat off Captain, I'll doctor you. Doc's a good barber and undertaker but I treated as many gunshot wounds as he did."

With a quick twist of his pocketknife, the slug popped out. He washed the wound with whiskey and wrapped the arm in a clean bar towel."

"I'm sorry, Captain," said General Custer.

"Don't fret over it, General. I can embellish about this wound the rest of my life."

"We'll sit over here," Mister Hickok said as he took General Custer by the arm and led him to the back corner of the saloon. He moved the table and placed two stools against the wall. He motioned me to join them, indicating a stool on the other side of the table. I sat there but kept looking back over my shoulder.

Mister Hickok laughed. "Don't worry, young pard, you have the two deadliest shots in the West covering you. Maybe our friend Bill Cody might disagree. George, I'd like you to meet my young friend here, Francis..."

"...Francis? Isn't that a girl's name?" General Custer said with the obligatory smirk.

"...Francis Scott Roche, named for that great American. He's writing my biography. Don't pull a face, George. It won't

6

be that bunk of Ned Buntline's. It will be the real truth. Francis Scott is educated. He's a graduate of the Pennsylvania University."

"Pennsylvania State College."

"I spoke at that great institution," General Custer said. "It's in Philadelphia."

"No. It's in the middle of Pennsylvania. It's near…Well…it's not really near anything."

"Libby and I plan to visit Philadelphia to celebrate the Centennial. I was to be a speaker. That is, before the…before the…I'll make a point to visit your alma mater. Maybe I could…"

I let General Custer go on and on. No use trying to correct him. He never heard of the Pennsylvania State College. Not too many people had. The school used to be the Agricultural College of Pennsylvania. Now there's engineering, mining, teaching, and, for the new female co-educational students, home economics.

"…Yes, fine school. Some of my officers…" General Custer stopped his rambling long enough to peer at me. "You look familiar. Did you ever meet me?"

"Yes, Sir. Early in June. I requested to go on your campaign as a correspondent."

"Obviously I didn't grant that request. For that you can be thankful. If only I had refused my two brothers, cousin and brother-in-law…" Then turning to Mister Hickok, "Christ, Bill, why couldn't I have been killed with my command? I would have been a hero now. A hero, not a goddamn…"

"George, my good friend. Brother. Don't be so hard on yourself. We'll get the truth known. But you just mentioned a very good idea. We'll all visit Philadelphia for the Centennial Exposition. But right now…"

Gunshots rang out. General Custer and Mister Hickok were on their feet with drawn pistols.

"Take that you no good son-of-a-bitch," rang out a rough voice from the outside. More gunshots followed. More yelling."

"It's that goddamn Martha Jane Cannary," shouted Jerry Lewis as he ran through the front door. "She's shooting up Jack McCall's corpse."

"No, no, not Martha Jane," Mister Hickok said as he holstered his revolver, sat down and took his head in his hands.

"I see you and Martha Jane are at it again," General Custer said with a lustful leer.

"Me and that...that...that...were never at it and you very well know that, George. She may be a poke for you but some of us has principles when it comes to certain women."

I don't believe this Bill. What happened to you? It wasn't long ago that you'd poke a pile of rocks hoping there'd be a snake inside."

"Well, times change. A man has to..."

"Mister Hickok's a respectable married man now, General," said Harry Young, also with a lustful leer.

"Married! What the hell difference does that make?" General Custer said almost in astonishment. "That should never stop a man. If I..."

"Bill, darling, you're alive, alive," said the large homely woman known as Calamity Jane, who was now running a straight course to Mister Hickok. "They said you were dead: that Broken Nose Jack shot you in the back. But don't worry. I kilt him good."

Before Mister Hickok had a chance to defend himself, she jumped into his lap and kissed him. The stool broke and they landed on the floor.

Mister Hickok jumped up spitting and wiping his mouth. "Don't do that again ever or I swear I'll shot you." He reached out his arm and Harry Young placed a large glass of whiskey in his hand. He took a mouthful, swished it around, and then expectorated it neatly into the nearest spittoon.

I leafed though a tablet. Mister Hickok married Agnes Lake this past March 5. After a two-week honeymoon he left her in Cincinnati and headed West for the new gold fields, which was where he was heading before he got married.

Mrs. Hickok was the owner of the Lake Circus. She was a famous equestrienne, queen of the high wire and one of the first females to enter a cage of wild animals. No doubt of it, she was quite a woman. She was also quite a bit older than Mister Hickok, ten or eleven years. From the tintype Mister Hickok carried, she looked it."

"Hello, General," Calamity Jane bellowed out, her normal tone of conversation. "Heard you got in town. You look even more handsome than ever with your hair grown back. I don't believe any of that bunk they're saying of you. Anyone calls you a coward will get shot by me. They know that so they don't say anything when I'm around. Nor when Bill's within earshot. You're the bravest man around. You and my Bill and Bill Cody. The real cowards are that Reno and Benteen. Those bastards kilt the Seventh. They should be..."

"Thank you Martha Jane, I knew I could always count on you," General Custer said, bestowing upon her his lustful leer. "Maybe tonight you could tell me more about..."

"I swear, George, you're the randiest man in the country," Mister Hickok said, "You have that lovely, sweet, dear creature and you are...by the way, where is Libbie now?"

"My dear wife Elizabeth is in Washington attempting to set straight this grievous injustice from the political end. I still have many friends in high places. Unfortunately President Grant isn't one of them. He hated me before this debacle at the Little Big Horn and hates me even more now. He knows he made a mistake by forcing me to resign and having his lackeys' court martial me. He threatened to have me shot if I didn't go along. He meant it. I was going to let him, but, Libbie...ahh...you know. But when the people finally learn the truth, they'll be shooting him. Him and those other conspirators in the Army who are protecting their butts. I know I won't get the truth out of them. The only living who knows the truth are Crazy Horse and the Sioux. But who'd believe them? Maybe some..."

"Calm down, old pard," Mister Hickok said as he placed an arm around General Custer's shoulder. "You're with friends now." Cheers from the patrons, which had swelled considerably since the shooting.

"We'll turn around this injustice. But for now. Let's eat."

With that, two of the biggest steaks I had ever seen were placed before the General and Mister Hickok. Harry Young brought a bottle of port to the table and exhibited the label to the Legends of the West. All nodded approval. The bartender carefully removed the cork and filled crystal glasses.

"Martha Jane. Guard the door and don't let anyone in but friends. General Custer and I want to have a quiet meal."

"Yes, Bill, anything you want," Martha Jane said almost demurely. And in a voice loud enough to be heard in Lead City, "Shut up you yahoos. Mister Hickok and General Custer want a quiet meal."

A steak was set before me; perhaps an afterthought, but I wasn't complaining. I almost had a fork in when...

"Carl! Take that steak away from Francis Scott. He needs room to scrivel. I want the record of the General's word right from the beginning."

And scrivel I did. I was certain Mister Hickok's meaning of "the beginning" was from the beginning of the military engagement at the Little Big Horn. General Custer began at the beginning of his life: the "humble" beginning as he called it.

Except for some extremely long periods of childhood, adolescence, young manhood, civilian and military injustices, and sloppy sentimentality of the same periods, it was an interesting story. I would have felt fortunate just listening to it, as was half of Deadwood now doing, but I had to write it.

Harry Young kept finding new tablets and writing implements to imprint this vast storehouse of information. My fingers had long ago gone numb and during those brief periods when the General was shoving another piece of steak into his mouth (he and Mister Hickok had eaten several) or washing it down with wine (the fine port was history, it was now the bar jug). I had to bite my writing fingers to get feeling from them.

During some of the extended periods of outrageous indignation or puerile mawkishness, members of the audience tried to sneak out. They quickly discovered they were a captive audience. Once in the No, 10, there was no out. Martha Jane saw to that. Even pleas of "Come on, Calamity, if I don't piss my bladder will bust," fell on unsympathetic ears.

10

General Custer at last got to that foggy dawn on May 17 when the Seventh U.S. Cavalry headed west from Fort Abraham Lincoln.

"As I led those gallant troopers to spearhead a campaign to drive those hostiles once and for all to their reservations, the band struck up my battle hymn, 'Garryowen.' It brought tears to my eyes. But you will have to wait to hear the stirring conclusion. I have to go out back and shake the snake. Har, har."

With that the General and Mister Hickok ran out the back door. The patrons, to a man, ran out the front door sweeping Martha Jane along in the stampede. It sounded as if rain were falling. Please let the General have a lengthy urination.

The piss call gave me an opportunity to examine my scriveling. All of it but the parts I had marked by folding a corner of a page.

It took a war to bring together General Custer's fabled blend of rashness, bravery and luck. If the object of war, as General Sherman said, is to produce results, General Custer's rashness, or as many have said, recklessness, couldn't be faulted. He lost more men during the Civil War than any other commandant. There was no arguing how fearless he was in a charge. Eleven horses were shot out from under him. Yet he came through the war unscathed except for a graze of shrapnel, a touch of influenza and a poison oak infection.

His rapid promotion—his first star at twenty-three, the youngest American ever to win one—was a surprise to friend and foe alike. This leadership certainly didn't show up at West Point where he graduated thirty-four in a class of the same number, and accumulated 726 skins, far higher than the runner up of demerits. The General pointed out that the top member of that class of 1861 was Patrick Henry O'Rorke who was killed at Gettysburg, so there is no telling how famous he might have became.

General Custer often told future cadets of West Point to study his record and avoid his example.

After the war, he was mustered out of the volunteer army. The $8,000 paid as a major general was reduced to $2,000 as captain in the regular army. He was given 4,000 Troops and sent

11

to Houston, Texas, to remind those in the Southwest just who won the war.

To say he was a stickler for discipline would be a gross understatement. Minor infractions were answered with flogging, a disciplinary measure prohibited by Congress in 1861. He was always a man of contrasts. On Christmas Day of 1865 he wore a Santa Claus suit while distributing gifts to his staff.

Between his actions and his mouth, General Custer managed to keep the pot of controversy boiling. In the summer of 1867, he was found guilty of going over the hill after he left his command to visit Libbie. This journey, no matter how romantic, was not considered a necessary trip. For this and other charges, including ordering deserters shot on the spot, he was suspended from his rank and command for one year and forfeit of pay.

He considered the sentence an outrageous injustice yet admitted if it wasn't for his war record; he might have been dishonorably discharged. But he survived and repaired the homestead back in Monroe, Michigan, to go out and fight another day.

It was his mouth, though, that almost kept him out of his last battle. He had been expected to command the entire army out of Fort Lincoln, not just the cavalry, when he really pissed off President Grant. With a lack of prudence, he testified against the President's Secretary of War, William Kelknap, who was accused of taking bribes, not exactly a rarity in the Grant administration. Also, General Custer couldn't keep it under his hat that he didn't care much for the President's brother, Orvil, another with his palm poised skyward. Grant was honest but very sensitive of criticism of his pack of thieves. Thus he forbade General Custer to join the campaign.

It was only after much ass kissing by generals Terry and Sheridan that Grant allowed him to go.

As the General and Mister Hickok returned, I began feeling traces of life in my scriveling hand. The saloon was again filled. Martha Jane again shouted for everybody to shut up.

"Let's see, where was I?" General Custer pondered. "Did I get as far as my days in West Point?"

The audience would have surely bolted if it weren't for Martha Jane and her brace of horse pistols.

"You were leading the Seventh out of Fort Lincoln and the band was playing 'Garryowen,' " shouted Harry Young.

"Yes, 'Garryowen.' I ordered the Seventh to circle the parade ground for the men to have one last chance to say goodbye to their wives or sweethearts. Or both. Har, har. Then the band struck up 'The Girl I Left Behind,' a poignant tribute to those brave women at the fort, including my darling Elizabeth."

Again the General failed to stick to a straight course. But, again, some of the digressions were fascinating. I scriveled furiously.

Included in the two-mile caravan of soldiers, artillery and white-hooded mules drawing wagons, were the General's four staghounds. The Custers were great lovers of animals. At Fort Lincoln, they kept about forty dogs and various wild and half-wild creatures including a pelican and a porcupine that sometimes slept on their bed.

The General also kept his sense of humor, rough as it was, on the campaign. One time all three Custer brothers were riding ahead of the column. As they passed through a ravine, Boston stopped to remove a pebble from his mount's shoe. The General and Tom kept riding.

As soon as they got out of sight, they dismounted, climbed a small hill, and, peering over the edge, saw Boston. The General shot over his head, knowing Boston would think it was Sioux. Boston jumped on his horse and galloped back to the column. His brothers rolled on the ground laughing.

There was also time for souvenir collecting on Indian burial grounds. A warrior's burial scaffold was found near where the Tongue and Yellowstone rivers converged. The vertical supports, painted red and black to show the deceased had been brave, were pulled down and the troops were allowed to help themselves to the funeral paraphernalia; beaded moccasins, rawhide bags, horn spoons and the like. The Negro interpreter Isaiah Dorman threw the stripped corpse in the river. The General suspected Dorman used the flesh as bait.

Finally, forty days and four hundred miles later, the Seventh reached a stark ridge above the Little Big Horn in Montana Territory. It was from this location that he saw the tepees of an Indian village. It was here he divided his command. Captain Frederick W. Benteen was given one hundred and fifteen troopers and was to scout the Indians from the southwest. Major Marcus A. Reno, with one hundred forty troopers, was to attack the village's southern end. And the General, with five companies, two hundred and ten men, rode north for a few miles along the ridge paralleling the village.

"The armchair generals are saying I underestimated the size of the village and the number of warriors. I knew from my scouts there were more than 1,500, maybe even 2,000 warriors in the village. These armchair generals are also saying I shouldn't have divided my command. They conveniently forgot this was West Point tactics. I used the same tactic in Oklahoma when I destroyed Black Kettle's village. In my mind, Sitting Bull's village was no different. It was my decision and the right decision at the time. If only...if only..."

The General's voice broke. Mister Hickok reached out and gently took his arm.

"That's enough for now, old pard."

"No. I must go on. I want the world to know the truth. You back there," General Custer said as he struck a theatrical poise, stuck out his arm and pointed an elegant finger at the man in the rear of the crowd. The man was dressed as if he were on a stroll up the Broad Way in New York. He was also scriveling with a fury.

"You Henry Morton Stanley, the famous newspaper correspondent." This was uttered with unconcealed sarcasm. "You, who I wouldn't allow to join these gallant men on the final campaign. You, who have spread scurrilous lies about me. No! No! Don't shoot him Martha Jane. Not just now. I want him to tell the world the truth. Do you sir have the capability of doing that?"

The famous correspondent, whose worldly reputation was deserved, had been in Deadwood awaiting General Custer's arrival. He condescendingly spoke to me on several occasions.

He proved to be pompous, patronizing and hopelessly enamored by himself. But he wasn't a bad person. He even promised if I gave him personal information on Mister Hickok, he would secure for me a journalist position on one of the big eastern newspapers. I had been around enough livestock at my alma mater to know bullshit when I saw it.

"Yes, General. I will tell the world the truth as I have done in my illustrious and much applauded career as the premier journalist in this country, and perhaps even…"

"Shut your yap, you bag of farts. General Custer is doing the talking," said Martha Jane, apparently not a fanatic of Mister Stanley. "You do the listening and make sure what you're writing is the truth…"

"General. You were saying you were on the ridge approaching the village," interjected Harry Young.

"Yes. I knew with the element of surprise and my military genius, the hostiles were mine. I would rout them and, if I didn't drive them back to the reservation, turn them right into the teeth of the guns of Terry and Gibson. I lead my five companies to the highest elevation. This should have been named Victory Hill. Unfortunately, it is etched in history as Last Stand Hill."

Before the General had a chance to meander into maudlin land, Harry Young quickly spoke up. "The highest elevation, General?"

"Yes. Yes. It was an excellent location to start my charge on the village. Riding from the high grounds would give me the momentum. My men would have the advantage of a clear field of fire if the warriors tried to intercept us. My troopers wouldn't have to fire through their own, as would the warriors on the lower ground.

"I sent runners with orders for Reno and Benteen to join my position on the high grounds. There is a time for dividing a command and a time to bring it together. I ordered the men to dismount and bring their mounts in prone position; I didn't want a passing scout to see our position. I told Tom and Miles Keogh to keep the status quo. There was a small grove nearby. I told them I would ride to it and return in a few minutes. I had to relieve myself and I didn't think it was proper to do so in front of my men," he added almost apologetically.

"As I approached the grove, I looked back and noticed a slight elevation had blocked my command from view. I felt no reason to be concerned. I would be returning momentarily. Then, not a hundred feet away, my nemesis, the man I should have killed when I had the opportunity, Crazy Horse stepped out of the grove.

"He looked at me with as much surprise as I must have displayed to him. Crazy Horse. The Oglala Sioux. The real battlefield general of this gathering of tribes. You must remember Sitting Bull was a medicine man not a warrior. He was the spiritual leader.

"Crazy Horse was the war leader. And there he was on foot, right in front of me. He was an impressive sight. He had a red-backed hawk mount tied to his head, wore strings of magic pebbles and had painted hailstones on this chest. Crazy Horse never neglected his talismans. He had luck and still has.

"I believed God had sent me this chance. All I had to do was kill the heathen son-of-a-bitch, tie his body to a pony and send it to the village. The sight would have broken the spirit of the hostiles. Even Sitting Bull would know it was bad medicine.

"Crazy Horse did not have a firearm. He must have read my intention because he drew a long knife and stood defiantly before me. I didn't draw my Colt. Instead I drew my knife. I would fight him on equal terms. I spurred Ole Bess and headed straight for Crazy Horse. I was close enough to see him smile when the explosion went off in my head.

"I at last regained consciousness; the searing sun in my eyes and a throbbing pain in my head. Before I could orient myself to where I was and what had happed to me, I felt a tugging at my boots and buckskins. It took great effort to focus my eyes. Then I saw the three squaws who were trying to disrobe me.

"I shouted and kicked and punched at them. They jumped back It was the first time I saw an Indian turn white. They acted as if they had seen a ghost. They drew knives and approached me again. I tried to rise but fell back. There was a pounding of hoofs. A rider jumped from a pony. He yelled and struck the squaws until they ran off. It was Crazy Horse. He was sweated, covered with dust and had streaks of blood on his arms.

"I reached for my revolver. It was gone. I reached for my knife. Gone too. I tried to rise. I couldn't. My head ached. I touched the right side of it and felt a large lump under my hair.

" 'Your yellow hair saved you, General,' Crazy Horse said and gave an odd laugh. He held a canteen—an Army canteen— to my lips and I drank until I couldn't drink anymore. That tepid river water tasted better than the finest French wine. He poured the remainder of the canteen water over my head. It began to clear. The pain even began to subside.

"Crazy Horse took my head in his hands and examined it. 'I have not yet thanked the brave who threw the stone that saved me. Fortunately for you, it was only a glancing blow. It didn't break your skull but gave you a mighty lump. All Indians say you have a special god looking over you. He is still smiling at you.'

"He helped me to my feet. He held me steady until my head cleared again. He smiled as he ran his fingers over my hair. 'Every brave would be honored to have this scalp. But not this day, General. My people will not harm you on these sacred grounds. We leave now,' he said as he mounted his pony. 'Someone will follow us to seek revenge. It will not be you. You live but you will wish you had died.'

"He rode off. A half dozen braves joined him, all hooting, laughing and pointing repeating Winchester and Henry carbines at me. I fought confusion as I walked back to my command. My heart grew heavier and heavier as I realized a terrible tragedy lie ahead.

"As I came nearer, I saw what looked like white boulders scattered about. I then realized it was my men stripped by the hostiles. I approached closer and saw the bodies were horribly mutilated. This savage rage was even inflicted upon the horses. They were slashed and cut. Some were living, but breathing their last.

"One horse was still standing. Clutching the reins was Miles Keogh. He was stripped like the other troopers but he was not

17

mutilated. I knelt and took his other hand in mine. 'I'm sorry, Myles. I should never have left you men.'

" 'Don't blame yourself, George,' Keogh said weakly. This was the first time he had called me by my Christian name. I said nothing of this familiarity. 'You aren't to blame. The blame should go to those bloodsuckers in Washington. The hostiles came at us with repeating rifles. If we had repeating rifles, we could have held them off. Hell, George, we could have run them off. We could have killed every one of those heathens. I ask you, how is it those penniless savages can afford Winchesters and Henrys and all the rich government of these United States can afford are Civil War Springfield single shooters?'

" 'Please, Myles, what can I do to ease your pain? Should I…'

" 'Now don't be worrying about me, George. My blood is just about leaked out. But, here, take Comanche," he said as he handed over the reins. 'I guess those heathens were afraid to take a horse from a deadman. Take this too, please.' Myles gave me his custom-made English pistol. 'Crazy Horse handed it back to me after emptying it. He said, as I was the last man to fall, I should be left to live to tell the story of the battle. Lucky for him there were no bullets in it or I would have put one through his head. But I'm glad you live, George. You can tell the world how the men died bravely, and how they could have lived bravely if they had weapons as good as the hostiles.'

"He began coughing. Blood seeped from the corners of his mouth. I quickly looked through Comanche's saddlebags for Myles' flask. An Irishman should not be without his drink in his moment of death. I held the flask to his lips. He took a deep draught. When he finished, he smiled and began singing:

" 'Let Bacchus' sons be not dismayed
But join with me each jovial blade
Come booze and sing and lend your aid
To help me with the chorus.'
"I joined him in the Seventh's anthem:
"Instead of Spa we'll drink down ale
And pay the reck'ning on the nail

18

No man for debt shall go to gaol
From Garry Owen in glory.'

"He died in my arms. There was no time for mourning. Or need. Myles Keogh died a brave soldier. I had to find my brothers. I had no hope of finding them alive but I was not prepared for the shock of seeing Tom for the last time. The Indians took out all their vengeance on this dear brave brother of mine, who was twice the recipient of the Medal of Honor in the Civil War.

"He lay face down but I knew it was him. On his arm was his fanciful tattoo of the American flag and his initials. His body was riddled with arrows and the back of his head smashed. I turned him over and saw his abdomen was slashed horizontally and vertically, his entrails hanging. His throat was cut and his scalp was torn off."

The General stopped talking and a wild, haunted look came to his eyes. I then realized I had been so captivated by the account I had stopped writing. I now tried to catch up. A quick glance around revealed everyone was captivated. Not a creature was stirring, not even a barfly.

"Why don't you skip that part for now and go on with the story," Mister Hickok suggested.

"Yes, yes," the General said. "I loaded Myles' pistol, the same weapon I'm holding now, the same weapon that saved my dear friend Bill's life, and dispatched the wounded horses. Comanche was also wounded—apparently a bullet went right through him and into Myles' knee—but it wasn't a fatal wound. Comanche would live. He would be a symbol of the spirit of the Seventh Cavalry.

"After making sure no one was alive, either man or horse, I led Comanche outside this circle of death and waited out of sight. I watched the Indians folding their teepees and dismantling the village. The Indians won this battle but I at least took comfort in the thought that they would be defeated forever.

"I expected Reno and Benteen to attack any minute. They did not. After awhile the fullness of the event fell upon me and, from what I learned later, I sat in a trance until of the troops of

19

Terry and Gibson arrived on the scene the next day. A scene of sickly, ghastly horror.

"I was immediately charged with leaving my command. Benteen and Reno, to save their bloated butts, testified they saw me riding from my command just as the hostiles began their attack from the other side of the hill."

"Kill those rotten sons-of-bitches" shouted Martha Jane. The chant was picked up by the patrons.

The General waved them silent.

"No, boys, they weren't the cause of the massacre. Reno may be a drunken incompetent and Benteen a backstabbing bastard, but I believe them to be brave men. They couldn't rejoin me for the same reason my two hundred and ten men needlessly lost their lives—they were out-weaponed by the hostiles. I'll say it now and I'll say it to my death. The blood of the Seventh Cavalry drips from the hands of that man in the White House and those thieves surrounding him. Anything for the almighty dollar is the motto of the Grant administration…"

"George, maybe you should sit down now," said Mister Hickok. "You don't want to aggravate the president any more than you have already."

"…The blood of those brave men are on President Grant's hands. He and his pack of jackals should be taken out and shot…"

"Please, George. Sit down!"

"…He and those thieves should be shot full of arrows like my dear brother Tom. Their bellies should be slit and their guts scooped out. Their scalps should be ripped from their heads. Their ballocks and cocks cut off with a dull, rusty knife and shoved down their throats…"

Mister Hickok pulled his friend back to his seat and clamped his finely shaped fingers over his mouth.

Too late. Henry M. Stanley bolted out the door, without a doubt to the telegraph office. By tomorrow, President Grant will read an embellished—as if it needed to be—account of General Custer's sentiments in the overblown style of America's premier journalist.

"God bless General Custer," shouted Harry Young.

The crowd responded with a cheer that lasted five minutes. When the God-blessings finally faded out, Harry Young said it would be a good time for one of Mister Hickok's Indian stories. All agreed. Something was certainly needed to cut the morbidity hanging in the air. Harry Young threw me a wink. I liked him. It was he who told me of Mister Hickok's intelligence and droll sense of humor.

And as I soon learned for myself, Mister Hickok was far from a brumous individual. He was a warm and compassionate man. Well, maybe not to the thirty-seven men he killed. But then he did mellow considerably.

Mister Hickok stood up. There was the devil in his eye and, under the luxuriant moustache, a smile on his lips.

"We all owe much to this brave man. This fearless Indian fighter. This son of the Stars and Stripes. This man the Indians in respect call Yellow Hair and Son of the Morning Star. The hostiles never had a more feared enemy or a more outstanding benefactor. And not one man would be standing in this saloon, nor would the town of Deadwood Gulch exist if this man had not discovered gold in the Black Hills in Seventy-One."

Although Mister Hickok, as they say in vaudeville, was on a roll, his last remark overflowed with sarcasm.

"Yes, Deadwood Gulch, the town where everyone is greedy. The town filled with opportunists, full of rough characters, cutthroats, back-shooters, gamblers, and the devil's agents. You dregs of humanity should be busting with pride that this great American chose our Deadwood—no matter how wretched it may be—to tell the true story of what happened at the Little Big Horn. This is undoubtedly the biggest honor any of you scum will ever receive in life. This is a day you will never forget. And I want every man to go out in the world and spread the truth. Now let's hear our appreciation for General George Armstrong Custer."

Again the audience burst into applause and whistles. Mister Hickok used this time to down a shot of whiskey. He made a motion with his finger indicating I should keep writing.

"Now I'm going to tell you boys one of my prize stories," Mister Hickok said as he motioned the crowd to quiet down."

"I was scouting for General Custer," he said and swept his arm in the direction of the man himself. Another outbreak of applause. "I was scouting for General Custer some years ago in the Indian Territory. We were getting into southwestern Kansas, which was new country to me at the time. I was riding a distance ahead of the General's command when I saw an opening about two feet wide that appeared to run into a bluff.

"I decided to explore it. This passageway was about ten feet long and led to a large open space of considerable area surrounded on all sides by a wall. I thought to myself what a great protection from Indians this would be if one were hard pressed—the entrance being so narrow one could secrete himself on the inside and kill any number of them, since they could only enter one at a time.

"I was armed with a six-shooter and also a large knife. The thought had hardly passed through my brain, when in looking at the entrance I saw an Indian approaching. Knowing he was hostile I shot him. Another came and I shot him too.

"They kept coming one by one until I had discharged the six shots my gun contained. In those days we used the powder and ball six-shooters with caps on the nipples. Not having any ammunition on me, I was unable to reload. More Indians kept coming. I then drew my knife from my belt and backed up against the wall at the farther end, while in the meantime the open space became crowded with Indians."

Mister Hickok stopped his narrative. The saloon was quiet with apprehension. No one spoke. No one moved. Finally:

"What did you do then, Bill?" asked Harry Young, Mister Bones to Mister Hickok's interlocutor.

Mister Hickok hesitated for a moment.

"What could I do? There were so many of them, well armed, and I had only my knife."

"Well, then," questioned Harry Young, "what did they do?"

Mister Hickok gave a long sigh.

"By God, they killed me, boys."

The quiet continued. Finally, Harry Young began to laugh. He was joined by General Custer. Then the partners Mann and Lewis. Finally, the crowd burst into laughter.

It is doubtful if anyone in the saloon had ever seen General Custer laughing or smiling in any of his many portraits or photographs. Now he was laughing so hard tears were flowing from his eyes. Probably the first good laugh he had in many a moon. When laughing he looked boyish, much younger than his usual dour demeanor.

Just as the laughter began to die down, several rapid firing shots were heard outside.

"Take that you murdering son-of-a-bitch," a hoarse voice yelled. Several more shots followed.

Mister Hickok drew his ivory-handled Army Colts from their holsters so fast that if one blinked he would have missed the movement. Just as fast, when he heard the voice, they were reholstered.

"I kilt that back-shooting bastard. He was all hunched up on the porch waiting to sneak in and shoot someone else in the back," Colorado Charlie Utter declared as he ran into the saloon. "Oh, shit," he added as he looked around the crowded room. Every man, jack, woman, boy there, save Mister Hickok had a gun pointed at him.

"Don't get excited, boys. Put them away. It's only Colorado Charlie, my mostly silent partner," said Mister Hickok. "What the hell are you doing here now, Charlie? You were supposed to stay out camp to keep an eye on things until we filed our claim."

"You're alive. Alive," Colorado Charlie yelled as he rushed through the crowd to Mister Hickok and held him in a bearhug.

"Get away from me, Charlie, you smell like you fell in a still," Mister Hickok said as he shoved Charlie away and into General Custer, who shoved him towards me. I stepped aside and let him fall to the floor.

"Those sons-of-whores," Charlie yelled, still sitting on the floor. Noticing the women in the saloon, he tipped his hat and added, "Excuse me ladies. Those sons-of-bitches. That goddamn Tim Brady and Johnny Varnes. They told me you were dead. They told me Jack McCall shot you in the back."

"I'm afraid the reports of my death are greatly exaggerated. But what were you doing with those yahoos? You know they're trouble-makers and I don't want you around them when I'm not around."

"They came to camp, Bill. I was getting ready to come into town to file the claim."

"When, Charlie, when?" General Custer snapped.

"Godalmighty, General Custer himself. The coward of..." Charlie stopped after a well placed kick in his haunch by Mister Hickok. "...Ahh...I never believed those dirty lies that you ran away from your men. I never thought for a minute..."

"Shut up, Charlie," Mister Hickok said as he lifted his partner from the floor by the neck. "I know you did a lot of drinking—I can even smell it in this saloon—but don't embellish. Just answer the General's question. When did they tell you this bunk?"

"Let's see. I looked at the sun; it was about two hours after noon. I was saddling up the mule when they rode up. They asked me where was I going. I told them I had to see you about the claim. They said don't bother. You'd been shot by Jack McCall. I knew he'd have to shoot you in the back. I knew..."

Mister Hickok and General Custer looked at each other.

"We better take another look at Broken Nose before Doc Peirce plants him," Mister Hickok said.

"Stay with us," he said over his shoulder. "I want all of this on the record."

"Looks like a sieve," Doc Peirce said as he lifted the corpse by the hair to a sitting position. "Some of these shots could have been fatal," he added, poking a finger into the riddled chest, "but they weren't necessary. The one in the back of the head killed him instantly. I'd say just the right part of the brain to paralyze him. He wouldn't even been able to squeeze the trigger on reflex. That's the General's shot," he threw a salute at General Custer. "He saved your life, Bill."

"That's what he's suppose to do, Doc. Besides his wife would never forgive him if he allowed 'one of the most perfect types of physical manhood' to be shot in the back in his presence," said Mister Hickok with a wide smile.

The reference was from General Custer's book Life on the Plains. "Whether on foot or on horseback he was one of the most perfect types of physical manhood I ever saw." Missus Custer even did better in her writing. "Physically, he was a delight to look upon." Fortunately, Mister Hickok was a modest man and never allowed himself to be amoured by things said or written about him.

"Keep it up, Bill, and maybe next time..." General Custer said with an equally wide grin.

"Yes, sir, General. A perfect shot," Doc Peirce said as he threw a blanket over the body and motioned a man in the wagon by the dirt sidewalk to help him. "You did the town, hell, the territory, a favor by plugging this...this..." And lifting the blanket for another look, "ugly bastard. He's the most repulsive-looking man I've ever laid eyes on."

No protests came forth.

There was a hissing sound from the circling crowd that seemed directed at me. It was Mister Stanley motioning with his eyes and eyebrows.

"What do you want, Mister Stanley?"

"Shh, shh, shh," the great journalist shhed and again motioned with his eyes and eyebrows.

I made the two steps towards him, looking back and continuing to take down the conversation going on over the body.

"My young colleague, do you think it would be all right for me to step over and examine the body. For the record, of course, not just morbid curiosity. I mean, do you think Mister Hickok or General Custer are looking with unfavor towards me? After all, I am only an honest scribe doing his duty for this newspaper, his publisher, his career and the great American public."

"Certainly, sir. Doc Peirce wouldn't mind and I'm sure Mister Hickok and General Custer aren't angry with you. At least they aren't now. But after the story you telegraphed to the New York Herald makes its way to President Grant and the wire service, I'm not sure. Maybe, Sir, it would be to your advantage to book a ticket on the Deadwood stage."

"I know you're jostling me, young man; another habit you acquired from your mentor, along with cultivating a moustache and growing your hair long. But I know you wouldn't want to see such a prestigious and prominent personage as myself brutally assaulted for giving my readers what they desire."

I wasn't as certain on that point as Mister Stanley as I wrote down the conversation behind me and listened to the conversation in front of me. I knew Mister Stanley wasn't really afraid. He had fought on both sides in the Civil War and fought the aborigines across the African continent.

"Besides, we members of the Fourth Estate, no matter how unequal we may be, must present a united front. You, of course, realize I could advance your career tremendously. I could maybe even include you in my entourage when I leave again for Africa on the request of Leopold the Second of Belgium. But before we discuss anything else, I would like to peruse those many tablets you are keeping for Mister Hickok. I know many publishers and..."

"I don't think Mister Hickok would like that. He's writing his own memoirs and he's a little touchy on the subject. He recently threatened to shoot Edward Zane Carroll Judson if he wrote another Ned Buntline look on him. But I could ask."

"No, no. Don't bother. I must talk to the good doctor now," he said and stepped in front of the barber, undertaker and sometimes dispenser of medicine. "Doctor Peirce, I presume?"

"At least the bullets missed this," Mister Hickok said as he pulled a small string-drawn poke from the shirt pocket of the redundantly shot Broken Nose.

"Gold dust. Pretty hefty amount. How much do you make it to be, Bill?" asked General Custer.

"We could put it on the scale. But I'd say at least a hundred dollars."

"Just look at this bozo," General Custer said, planting his own kick to the haunch of the beyond complaining McCall. "He never had a hundred dollars together in his whole miserable life. You thinking what I'm thinking, Bill?"

"Certainly am, George. We're going to have to talk to those two yahoos. They may have spread some other dust around..."

"Bill, Bill. You're alive. Alive," yelled the man in fringe buckskins who just leaped from his horse and ran erratically towards Mister Hickok. Like Mister Hickok he had long hair and

26

a luxuriant moustache. He was Captain Jack, the poet scout and an intimate friend of Mister Hickok. He embraced Mister Hickok in a bearhug.

As with the last bearhug embracer, Mister Hickok shoved him away, "Godalmighty, Jack, you smell as if you fell in the same whiskey barrel as Charlie."

"Yes, my noble friend, I am three sheets to the wind. But it is because of despair. I learned of your demise and indulged myself with the nectar of the gods. The grape of..."

"Report, Captain," barked General Custer. "Who told you Bill was dead?"

"General Custer, Sir," snapped Captain Jack as he threw a snappy salute. "I am also in high spirits to see you alive," and drawing a Peacemaker—the latest revolver from Samuel Colt—from its holster, announced, "I'll shoot any scoundrel who even whispers those slanderous words, 'Coward of the Little Big Horn.' "

The General's eyes went wild and the right one again began to tick violently.

"Yes, we all know of your loyalty to the General," Mister Hickok said as he pulled Captain Jack to him and whispered in his ear, "Don't mention that 'Coward of the Little Big Horn' shit anymore. George is very touchy about that right this minute." And in his full voice, "Just report to the General."

"Sir," another snap to attention, another salute. "I was on my way to Bill's camp," and consulting a large railroad watch he pulled from his pocket, "about fifteen hundred hours, when I crossed paths with those despicable dastardly dregs of Deadwood, Brady and Varnes, I cleared my Peacemaker. Both threw up their hands. One or the other said, 'We ain't looking for trouble, Captain Jack. We're just going around alerting Bill Hickok's friends that he'd been shot in the back by Jack McCall.

"I was so stunned I just let them ride away. Dear Bill dead! Dear sweet Bill. Dear handsome Bill. The best friend a man..."

"Shovel that manure some other time. Go on with your report," Mister Hickok said.

"I rode as the wind to your camp. Not a soul was present. Colorado Charlie left a mournful note for me telling of your death. He also left half a jug of whiskey. Barely potable but at the moment it was the elixir of necessity. I sat and had a drink and decided to write your eulogy. I would have finished it if the jug had not of ran dry. I rode to town for further libation and saw you standing in front of the Number Ten; twice as big as life and twice, nay, trice as handsome."

"Honest, Jack, if you spread that manure on the fields back home in Troy Grove, the corn would be as high as a...a...a mastodon's eye."

"Bill, you cut me to the quick. I say all of this in sincere tribute to the greatest shootist who had ever lived. I must amend that. To the greatest living shootist."

"I thank you for that amendment," Mister Hickok said with a laugh, "but now I have to..."

"But what am I to do with this?" Captain Jack asked as he unfolded a large sheet of parchment. "This is the beginning of your eulogy. I guess I'll save it for another day."

"Much later, I hope," Mister Hickok said as he took the parchment from Captain Jack. After squinting at it for several seconds he handed it to me. "You read it, young pard, no use wasting all of Captain Jack's time and talent."

"I took the parchment and glanced at what appeared to be the first stanza of a poem. The penmanship was beautiful in the beginning but fell into distress as the poem progressed, undoubtedly the effect of the drink. I glanced over it again to make certain of the words.

"The title is 'The Burial of Wild Bill.' " Before I got any further, there were shouts to speak up. In a much louder voice, I began again.

"Under the sod in the prairie land
We have laid him down to rest,
With many a tear from the sad, rough throng,
And the friends he loved the best;
And many the heartfelt sigh was heard
As over the sward we trod,
And many an eye was filled with tears
As we covered him with sod!"

I paused. "That's all that's written now," I said as tears ran down my cheeks. Everyone had tears in their eyes; even the whores, who had the reputation of having the hardest hearts in the Black Hills.

"That's a very fine poem you wrote, Jack, and I'm touched. You make me feel like a slacker for being alive."

"Don't fret about it, Bill. I'll finish it when needed," Captain Jack said as he reached for the parchment.

"No, I think I'll keep it," Mister Hickok said as he carefully refolded the parchment and placed it in an inside pocket of his waistcoat. "I could use this in the book."

"Book? What book?" demanded Mister Stanley. "If you want a book, Sir, you surely know that I am the only person here, or in this country, impeccably qualified to take on a work of such magnitude. I have friends, I have connections, I have…"

"You have an asshole made of paper," Martha Jane said. "Bill can write his own book better than some weasel-worded fancypants from England."

"Madam, I resent your tone, your implications, your total lack of…"

"I ain't no madam. I never sold it in my life. See what I mean about you and your weasel words. I got a good mind to tell the General how you're going around town uttering that…"

"Miss Cannary, perhaps we could step inside and have a glass of wine," Mister Stanley said sweetly.

"What's that Martha Jane. What has he been saying?" the General snapped, his eyes beginning to get wild again.

"Let's forget that for now, dear friend. I have those two snakes to catch before they try to shoot me in the back themselves. If they found the courage for it."

"Let's round up a posse and run down those vermin," Colorado Charlie shouted. Everyone shouted in agreement.

"Gentlemen. If I may say a word please," Mister Stanley said. "The two men…vermin in question rode out of town earlier. I saw them making what I thought was an auspicious departure when I stepped into the telegraph office. I'm certain they are well on their way by now."

"No use worrying about them now, George. They're either holed up in the Hills or getting our of the territory."

"You're right, Bill; too much of a start," General Custer said and looking around added, "Besides this drunken lot couldn't find a buffalo with diarrhea. If I only had the Seventh. I'd ride them down and..."

"There's always tomorrow, dear friend. But the evening is still young. What do you want to do now?"

"Let's visit a whorehouse," General Custer said with a lustful leer.

"George, I'm a married man now. I'll be seeing my bride soon. Besides..."

"I've been married a lot longer than you and that never stopped me. I may be married but I'm not dead. Besides...what?"

"Besides the whores are all ugly. They're the ugliest bunch of whores I've ever seen in my life. But you know how that goes. Get a good-looking whore and a rancher with a big spread or a miner who hit paydirt marries her."

"You're jesting. Surely they couldn't be that ugly. Who'd pay?"

"Look around you," Mister Hickok said, flourishing an arm at the collection of Deadwood denizens surrounding them.

"I see what you mean, Bill," General Custer said disappointingly but quickly retrieved his enthusiasm. "What the hell. We could just visit. You never know. Maybe some new talent arrived."

"I don't know. I should play cards. We'll need money; not that this penurious lot has that much to lose."

"Play cards later. I've got a little soldier that needs close order drill," General Custer har-harred. But in a low somber voice, "Bill, ole pard, I need someone to watch my back and you're the only person I can trust my life to. They're all after me. They all want to crucify..."

"O.K., George, just a visit. We're not staying all night." And to the collective crowd that began following they across the street, "Go back to Number Ten. Mister Stanley is setting up the house. Isn't that right, Mister Stanley?"

"Certainly, Mister Hickok. The New York Herald can spring for a round."

"Or two."

"Or two," Mister Stanley said and in a majestic wave of his arm, "Follow me men," and marched majestically to the saloon, followed by the unmajestic mob.

"Not you Martha Jane," Mister Hickok said. "Guard the door. We don't want to be disturbed."

"Anything you say, Bill."

"I know I don't have to tell you, but keep a sharp eye and open ear for any news of Brady and Varnes, or any of their pardners."

"Now I better understand why they call this pustule on the carbuncle on the rump of civilization Deadwood," General Custer said as he crossed the narrow street filled with stumps, boulders, lumber and logs.

"It won't be necessary to write down everything," Mister Hickok said as he draped an arm over my shoulder. "Just the historical facts," he added with a wink. "Maybe it would be a good idea to put away your tablet. The world doesn't need to know every little detail. Come along anyway, you can talk to your little girlfriend."

The "girlfriend" was the daughter of one of the whores, actually the madam. She was just a little kid, about thirteen. She wasn't for sale nor would she ever be, according to her mother, who guarded her like, well, a whore guarding her money.

Her mother was quite attractive for an older woman. She was about thirty-five. She and Mister Hickok had some sort of relationship, which apparently went back a long way. He, however, never bothered to enlighten me about it.

The mother encouraged me to spend time with her daughter, no doubt under the assumption I was intelligent because I was a college graduate, a common mistake made by people who had never attended college.

I was teaching the little girl in the sciences, humanities and the arts. I rather enjoyed it. There was classroom work and field trips. She was a very smart child and I had to be alert to keep ahead of her. He mother had warned me she'd cut off my

31

ballocks if I tried to take advantage of her. Actually, the problem was the other way around. The daughter was an unmerciful tease and didn't miss an opportunity to take advantage of me.

"Yes, I should meet with Kit. We have some lessons to review and it would give me the opportunity to go over her poetry, prose and punctuation."

"Just as long as you don't go over her pussy," Martha Jane cackled. "Kittie has this big knife all sharpened up…"

"Better heed Martha Jane," Mister Hickok said as we crossed the street to the doorway where the General was tapping his foot. "Kittie would kill anyone who touched her Kit. In fact, I'd probably do it myself. Now don't say anything to George about Kittie. I'll run in and shove her in her room. I love George like a brother, but…"

"Move it out, Bill. Just smelling this whorehouse makes me horny."

"Stand fast, George. I'll reconnoiter for…" Mister Hickok yelled over his shoulder as he rushed through the whorehouse door with two drawn Colts. Screams could be heard followed by laughter.

"What did he say?"

"Ahh…he wants to make sure there are no…ahh…Indians around."

"Indians?"

"Yes…ahh…Indians. Mister Hickok doesn't want anyone ambushed by Indians."

"O.K., General, I've scouted the whorehouse," Mister Hickok said from the doorway. "No Indians in sight."

"Indians?" General Custer repeated as he shook his head and marched into the whorehouse.

Whores were sitting, standing and sprawling about the large parlor. All smiled as General Custer, which was unfortunate because half of them didn't have front teeth. Several had Seventh Cavalry guidons—the famous swallow-tailed flag with gilt stars—tattooed on their arms. One whore pulled up her gown to show the General the guidon tattooed on her buttock.

The General looked pleased and flashed his obligatory lustful leer. "How could you say these whores are ugly, Bill? They're..."

Mister Hickok studiously stared at the ceiling as whores turned to glare at him.

"...They're...they're...the flower of American whorehood," the General graciously announced. And in an aside to Mister Hickok. "I have to agree with you. They are ugly."

I felt a hand groping my buttock. I tried to ignore it. I didn't want to turn around and face an ugly whore. Then the hand slid to the front of my trousers and grabbed my... "Hey, hold it now," I said as I turned around and looked down into the face of Kit, the pretty, innocent face of Kit. There were times she looked very attractive and very unchildlike.

"Please, don't, Kit. Your mother will cut it off if she sees you holding it. Besides..." She squeezed a little harder. "Besides..." I couldn't think of another besides.

"Mother said you shouldn't hang around the whores; you have to give me my lessons. She's not here now. Bill shoved her in her room and told her to stay there as long as General Custer is here," Kit whispered and giggled. "I guess he doesn't want to share."

"That's a good idea, Francis Scott," Mister Hickok said from across the noisy room. I wasn't sure about his eyesight but there certainly wasn't anything wrong with his hearing. "Take Kit to her room and review her lessons. A whorehouse parlor is not the place for such a sweet young miss."

"You heard Bill, Franny," Kit said as she wrapped her arm in mine and led me to the hallway and the row of rooms.

We entered a room at the end of the hall. Kit sat on the small, narrow bed and motioned me to sit next to her. I chose a chair in the far corner, which wasn't that far away considering the room was so small.

"O.K., Kit, where are your books?" The walls were so thin I could hear the conversation in the parlor. It was mostly General Custer doing the talking and the whores doing the laughing. "I hope you finished your last lesson. Today I will teach you..."

"Franny, I don't want you to teach me anything from the books. I want you to fuck me. I'm tired of being a virgin," Kit said and began opening the buttons on her blouse.

"Ahh...well...Kit...geewiz...you know how your mother...don't take off any more clothes...no Kit...put your skirt and drawers back on...I can't...I can't...your mother will...Oh, God, you have a beautiful body, Kit."

I stared in awe at Kit's nakedness. In clothes she looked like a skinny little girl. Or maybe because she was a little girl I never looked at her closely. But I was looking now. Her breasts were full and stood erect. Their pink nipples were surrounded by fainter pink aureoles about the size of silver dollars. Her flat abdomen curved inward and revealed a large narrow navel. Her hips flared softly into shapely legs. And those buttocks.

"Wow...gosh...Kit...I...I...I...But your mother...I better go." But I made no effort to leave. I just took in the scenery.

"Don't worry about mother. Bill will keep her busy for awhile. Now get over here right now and fuck me. What are you a sodomite or something?"

"No, no. I'm not a sodomite. I'm just afraid..."

"Franny, get over here right now or I'll start screaming and tell mother you raped me."

"Don't scream, Kit. I'm coming," I said as I quickly undressed and jumped into the bed.

"Be gentle," she said as she kissed me, almost sucking out my lungs. "But for chrissake hurry up."

Everything was one big sensation. Flashes of lightning going off in my head thunder going off in my body and electricity in my limbs. I couldn't believe it, as I at last was unable to continue.

"You're not stopping already, Franny? Are you? We just got started."

"It's been four or five times. Maybe when I catch my breath."

"I love you, Franny," Kit said as she wrapped her arms around me tightly and kissed me."

"I love you too, Kit. I think." I sprung up quickly, almost dumping her from the bed. "But godalmighty you're just a child. They put men in prison for this stuff."

"Don't believe that bunk of my mother's," she said and laughed. "I'm not a little girl. I'm seventeen years old, a woman. My mother says that and makes me dress in these baggy clothes to keep the customers away. At least that's what she says." Another laugh. A throaty lovely laugh. "But I think she's just trying to hide her real age. As long as I'm a kid. She's still young. If it's up to her, she'll probably try to keep me a kid the rest of my life. So, really, you have nothing to worry about, Franny."

"That makes me feel good. That and, well, what we just did. But will you do me one little favor?"

"I'd do anything for you. Haven't I already." Another laugh.

"Please don't call me Franny. It sounds so sissy-like."

"I can't call you Francis Scott; that's too long. By the time I say your name I'll forget why I said it."

"Yea, it is pretty long. And it's pretty sissy-like too. Why couldn't I have a name like the men around here? You know, Bill, George, Harry, Carl, Jerry, Charlie or even Jack. No, I have to be Francis Scott."

"Maybe I could call you Scott?"

"No. That's just as sissy-like."

"I got it. I can call you F. Scott."

"What?"

"F. Scott. Your initial and second name."

"Hum, that sounds different. But no. Too literary."

"What do you want me to call you? Mister Roche?"

I even laughed at that one. "No, my father was Mister Roche. I'll tell you what. Call me Franny. But not when anyone else is around."

"Well, Franny, I'm glad that's settled," she said as she snuggled closer. "How you feeling? Think you're ready for another…"

Her words, the serenity and the sensuality were shattered by a loud, piercing voice, unmistakably Martha Jane's.

35

"Bill, your mama's out here and she wants to see you." Her announcement was followed by a loud cackle.

A door slammed open outside of our door and Mister Hickok's voice could be heard.

"What's that crazy woman yelling about now? Mother is home in Illinois. I just received a letter from sister Lydia. She wouldn't let mother travel here."

"There's an older-looking woman standing in the middle of the street," a female voice said.

"That's Mom," Kit said as she smiled and held me even tighter. "Don't try to squirm away. I'll scream."

"Here, Bill, look through the shutter. Do you see her?"

"I don't believe what I'm seeing. Agnes. Of all the times…"

"Agnes? Your wife? What's she doing here?"

"Damned if I know, sweet Kittie. But I better get dressed and sneak out the back. She has a frightful temper."

"I better warn Kit and Francis Scott. They're in there studying, you know," Kittie said as she opened the door to Kit's room.

"Hello, Mother," Kit said as she held on to me, preventing me from leaping out of the bed.

Kittie was stunned into silence. Her jaw hung almost to her bosum, a rather ample bosum. Standing behind her was Mister Hickok; buck-naked except for the pair of Colts holstered around his waist. His eyebrows shot up but he quickly recovered. A possum-eating-shit grin spread across his face and he threw me a wink.

"I'm going to kill…I'm going to cut…I'm going to…Give me a gun I'll shoot the bastard now," Kittie yelled when she finally got her voice back. Mister Hickok prevented her from entering the room."

Calm down, Kittie. We knew this had to happen sometimes. He's a good young man. Be thankful of that. But we can settle this later. We have more urgent business outside."

"You son-of-a-bitch, James," shouted Agnes in a voice loud enough to be heard in every corner of the big top. "You come out of that whorehouse right now or I'm coming in to get you."

"I'll kill him, Bill. Just take your hands off me. How dare he take advantage of my little child? She's practically an infant. It seems like yesterday she was suckling my breast."

"Let's not get too carried away, Kittie," Mister Hickok said and rolled his eyes.

"I'll cut off his…"

"Just the thought of it caused my ballocks to shrivel and try to retreat into my body.

"Oh, Mother, stop it, please," Kit said and laughed.

"Kittie, calm down. Agnes is banging on the front door now. I told you she has a frightful temper. Now get dressed, young man. If you can break yourself away. Kit! Quit rasseling him. We have to get out of here."

Another voice in the hall.

"What the hell's going on?" barked General Custer. Two whores, one uglier than the other, held onto him. He was also buck-naked except for the custom English pistol and knife around his waist. "A man can't even fuck in peace anymore."

"You get dressed too, little girl. I'll take care of you later," Kittie said as she closed the door to the room.

I was already dressing. I looked over at Kit's pretty face and lovely body and almost got excited again.

"Do you want to try a quick one?" Kit inquired.

Banging on the door.

"Let's go, stud," Mister Hickok yelled.

I completed dressing and came through the door, turning to give Kit a last look. "I love you," I mouthed. She did the same.

"Come out of there, you whoremaster," Agnes shouted. "Mister Stanley told me you are in there. I know he is too prominent of a journalist to lie."

I looked through the shutter and saw a smirking Stanley slither away.

"You stay here, Bill, I'll take care of this," General Custer said as whores helped him to dress as he walked to the parlor.

"Be careful, George, she has a temper like…"

"Don't worry about me, old scout. I laughed at the guns at Gettysburg. I single-handedly defeated…" General Custer's voice faded as he walked to the front door and opened it.

37

"Missus Hickok, you have been misdirected. You are the victim of a vicious prank. Your husband, a man of high moral character and practically a brother to me, is not on these premises. Go now and leave these hard-working whores in peace so they can carry on their profession."

"Get out of the way, you son-of-a-bitch or I'll break your neck too."

As General Custer tried to shove her away from the door, Agnes threw a roundhouse right that caught him on the jaw, knocking him to his ass halfway across the room.

The whores ganged up on her and shoved her outside. The door was quickly bolted.

"I'll be back," she shouted from the sidewalk as she walked away.

"I can't believe how strong that woman is," General Custer said as he arose, rubbing his jaw. "I believe, men, it is now time for a strategic withdrawal. I'll hide Bill in the Hills until his bride calms down."

Just then, shouting and thundering of hoofs. All rushed to the front window. Agnes Hickok, nee Agnes Lake, famous equestrienne, was on the back of a big mule that was galloping straight to the whorehouse.

"That's a freight line mule. I'll wager it never moved this fast in its life," Mister Hickok said with a touch of pride in his voice.

To the astonishment of everyone, the mule even picked up more speed as Agnes drove it right through the front door of the whorehouse. Clamoring, screaming and the breaking of wood could be heard as the three of us ran out the back door. Then from the security of the rear of the large crowd gathered, we observed the riding skills of this woman, who was also one of the first women to tame lions and tigers.

Whores ran out the front door as the breaking sounds continued inside. I was relieved to see Kit, tucking her blouse inside her skirt, run down the street.

"That's one happy young woman," Mister Hickok said. "It'll take a couple of days for both of you to get those smiles off your faces."

38

More breaking of wood and more clamors as Agnes brought the mule through a wall of the whorehouse. She spun the animal around and made it dance on its rear legs before riding it through another wall.

Another loud crack was heard. A portion of the roof caved in. The crowd fell silent but began cheering again as Agnes crashed the mule through the last standing section of wall. A second or two later, the rest of the roof collapsed.

The crowd cheered and applauded. Agnes smiled, stood on the back of the mule and made it prance. "

"A true trouper," Mister Hickok said.

"Yes, indeed. The finest display of mulemanship I have ever witnessed," General Custer said and added with a sad note in his voice, "But where are the poor whores going to live?"

TWO

Two weeks later, approaching high noon, gold claim camp, the Black Hills.

General Custer's worry about the habitat of the displaced whores was soon alleviated. Once Agnes was convinced that Mister Hickok was not in that whorehouse at the time, nor was he a frequenter of any other whorehouse (everyone in front of the No. 10 Saloon, with the exception of Broken Nose McCall, swore to that), she became repentant.

With the energy and skill required to raise the Big Top, and with the assistance of a small army of enthusiastic volunteers, she soon had the whorehouse back to its original condition. She also did a pass-the-hat performance of more of her equestrian skills and donated the money to the whores to buy new furniture and windows.

The result of all of this was that Mister Hickok, who really loved Agnes, in his manner, had to prospect for gold as he told her he was doing. He hated it; manual labor was not his forte. He hated it because he considered it undignified. But he hated it even more because it kept him away from the card table.

It was true that strikes were made and prospectors left the Black Hills with money. Most of the money came from mining consortiums that bought promising claims and had the finances to mine them.

But Mister Hickok knew his fortune was at cards. He mined the card table for those small pokes of gold dust, those couple of nuggets the less prosperous prospectors brought to town after a hard week's work in the Hills.

"This is no life for a man, Francis Scott," Mister Hickok lamented as he sat on the easy chair and rested his moccasins on a stump. He was dressed in spotless fringed buckskins and was oiling and tuning his weaponry, which included his legendary pair of pearl-handled Colt revolvers given to him by Senator Henry Wilson, a thirty-eight belly gun, a thirty-two boot gun, a forty-four/forty Winchester repeating rifle, a forty-five Henry repeater, a forty/seventy Sharps buffalo gun, and a custom Springfield sporter.

"Hold on, young pard, we shouldn't work so hard. Sit down for a couple of minutes. Grab that water crock while you're up."

Very dirty, very sweaty and clad in denim trousers so thoroughly dirt-encrusted they could stand by themselves, I walked over to the five-gallon crock, carried it to Mister Hickok, and handed him the dipper.

"Set it down, set it down. You don't have to stand there with it."

The crock was set on a stump next to Mister Hickok. I dropped onto another. My buttocks were scraping close to the ground. Because I once told Mister Hickok I had taken several mining courses at the Pennsylvania State College, I was put in charge of the actual mining operation.

I really knew very little—the courses were for coal mining not gold mining—but I soon learned that was a hundred times greater than the combined knowledge of Mister Hickok, General Custer and Colorado Charlie, partners of the Utter Gold Mining Corporation. Charlie had staked out the original claim and it rapidly became evident it was possibly the most barren claim in the Hills.

There was a saying that a blind man on a fast horse could find gold in the Black Hills. Maybe so, but not Charlie. There was gold to be washed out of streams or dug in the veins of ore, panned by miner's pans, sluiced in the wooden sluice boxes. All were tried but still no gold. But I couldn't complain; the pay was good, as were the fringe benefits.

"I didn't know marriage could be such a pain-in-the-ass or prospecting such hard work," Mister Hickok said with a sigh. "You might as well clean up. I want you to run a couple of

42

errands in town. Don't forget my note for George. You are working for him tonight, correct? And no doubt you might want to say hello to Kit."

Yes, that was certain. Despite seeing her several times a day for the past two weeks, I missed her when we weren't together. Although I no longer feared that her mother would kill me or do something even worse, I did keep out of her way and made sure I was never alone with her. Her mother, however, insisted that Kit still dress like a little girl, which didn't bother me. But I did learn from Kit that the reason this ruse was so successful was that Kit was a late bloomer. She really didn't start filling out until the past year, much to her chagrin.

I just happened to come around at the right time. The right time for Kit, who decided since deflowering had to be done eventually, she wanted me to do it. Neither Kittie nor Mister Hickok had any delusions I had seduced Kit. They knew it was the other way around.

The two of them also decided since it would be impossible to keep us apart, I could see her anytime. There was, however, a small hook, but a hook swallowed as quickly by me as a hungry trout swallowing a hook baited with a big worm. They had decided years ago that Kit would never go into whoring. But there was no reason to give it away. We could be lovers and make love as much as we wanted but I would have to pay the going rate.

To keep all of this on a higher moral level, no money would change hands in the whorehouse. Mister Hickok would keep the account up to date and I would owe him the money, which would be set aside for Kit's college education.

This arrangement delighted Mister Hickok and Kittie. It also delighted me until Mister Hickok handed me the first bill. I couldn't believe it. The first week cost me more money than my entire college education. How could anyone fuck that much? Looking back, I guess it was easy. Even Mister Hickok was somewhat taken back and suggested cutting back on the pussy and spending more time on the books.

But cutting back was not a good idea; making more money was. I was still a correspondent for several smaller papers in the

East. But as anyone who has ever taken up the pen for newspapers knows, they are notoriously cheap. Certainly Mister Stanley was making good money but he was more of a businessman who knew how to create a moneymaking story. But he was the exception. Most newspapermen worked for practically peanuts. Even those newspapers that proclaimed to be labor-oriented and preached for higher wages for the workie, didn't pay much attention to their own policy when it came to paying their own.

But then publishers of newspapers had long ago learned that correspondents and reporters would work for practically nothing—and at times even less than that—if they could see their work in print.

Newspapers were pioneers in bringing women to the non-industrial workplace. This wasn't because they believed in women's suffrage or equal rights for women. No, it was because they could pay women even less than men for the same work.

Fortunately, Mister Hickok paid generously. I also worked for General Custer, whose original talk on the real story of the Little Big Horn proved to be such a success that the proprietor of a local stage company arranged performances for him.

General Custer, as they say in the entertainment press, was boffo. He packed the house twice a day, seven days a week. My main job was to sell tickets and keep an eye on the gate. I was honored General Custer trusted me. I also arranged his talk in a script so he wouldn't digress or regress or ramble on which was his natural style. A side concession was selling autographed woodcut pictures of the General and Mister Hickok. Kit, who did most of the ticket selling, signed the autographs.

"Are you listening to me, Francis Scott? I want you to clean up and run some errands. I have notes for George and Agnes."

To keep up the charade for Agnes, Mister Hickok was staying at the claim camp with Charlie and myself. Although Agnes Hickok insisted her husband should prospect and not gamble, she had no intention of staying at the camp. And who could blame her? The camp consisted of a tent, a rough—very rough—log house, and a shithouse about three hundred yards away in the woods.

No, Agnes, circus owner and star, would not be caught dead in the camp. She stayed at the new hotel in Deadwood. And although it was the latest in Black Hills accommodations, she let it be known that even it was a hardship on her. She was used to much finer things.

General Custer also had a room at the hotel. Although he was a partner in the mining venture, he would not condescend to stay at the camp nor do any manual labor.

His wife's arrangements were fine with Mister Hickok since it allowed him to sneak in town as soon as it got dark. The partners in the No. 10 arranged a poker table in the back storage room where Mister Hickok played his beloved poker with select card players until sometimes after midnight. Then he would visit Kittie and spend the rest of the night with her.

That left Charlie and myself in camp. But Charlie was seldom around. He was either in the Hills looking for a more promising claim or whooping it up in Deadwood or nearby Lead City. So, it was usually up to me to secure the camp. I was usually gone as soon as I was alone. I knew that as low-life, craven and greedy as many of the local inhabitants were, none were stupid enough to steal from Mister Hickok's camp.

"Tell Agnes I won't be able to have dinner with her. Just too much work around here," Mister Hickok said as he took another sip of spring water, motioning me to pour more in his cup.

"Missus Hickok told me to tell you if you don't have dinner with her today, she'll end her visit and leave for civilization. She told me that last night and said I should repeat it three times. If you don't have dinner…"

"Yes, yes, I understand you. All I have to say is its about time. Now don't misunderstand me, I really care for that woman. Only I care for her in civilization, not here. Maybe I shouldn't have married so hastily. But I honestly thought it was a good idea at the time."

This was becoming a familiar story. Mister Hickok had been greatly impressed by Agnes Lake's talents in the circus. He compared her skills with horses, wild animals and the high wire with his of shooting. He had known her for three years and by chance met her again in Cheyenne on his way to the Black Hills.

45

They married but soon separated. The pull of the gold (on the card table) and the opportunity to be part of the last vestige of the frontier beckoned to him.

Civilization came too fast for Mister Hickok. The frontier, like the buffalo and Indian, was vanishing before his eyes. And here was Deadwood—not even recognized by the government because the land belonged to the Indians—perhaps his last chance to prolong the past.

"Do you think she'll really leave?"

"I think so. She said she should return to the circus before they steal her blind."

"Be it as it may. How is the General doing? We haven't crossed paths in a couple of days."

"His performance is excellent. Very bombastic, just like himself. The audience sits there in awe. I feel fortunate to be around such an historic personage. But he can be demanding. He keeps throwing orders at everyone. And especially me."

"Don't mind George. He's been a commanding officer so long he thinks everyone should snap to attention when he's around. And they usually do. As I mentioned before, be tolerant. These are dark times for him. He not only lost the Seventh, which he loved more than anything in the world, but has been branded as a coward. And him the bravest man in this country. George may be many things—headstrong, reckless, vain, glory seeking—but never a coward.

"George lost confidence in himself. You probably wouldn't know it, nor would most people, but I can see it. He blames himself for the massacre. His friends, you and I foremost, must do everything to help him. That is why I allowed him to save my life by shooting Broken Nose McCall."

"You allowed General Custer to shoot McCall? But your back was to him. How could…"

"Yes, my back was to him. I figured that was the only way I could get him to make his move on my terms. I didn't want to give him the opportunity to shoot me in the back on some dark night. I didn't survive as a lawman all of these years without being able to recognize a criminal type. There was too much coincidence; he was dogging by footsteps those last two days of

46

his life. Harry Young had tipped me off the Montana bunch wanted me dead. I reckoned they heard I was offered the job as marshal and…"

"Marshal? I didn't…"

"I didn't make up my mind yet. Even if I wanted it, I couldn't take the job until Agnes is out of town. Anyway, I knew someone was paying Broken Nose to kill me. The Montana gang, Brady and Varnes or maybe someone else who would lose money if there were law and order in Deadwood. That is why I sat with my back to the door. Broken Nose would have never made a move if I were sitting against the wall."

"But how did you…"

"Simple, young pard. Before the saloon opened that morning. I had Harry round up every mirror he could lay his hands on. I positioned them so I would have a three-hundred-and-sixty degree view of my back. I knew Charlie Rich would take my usual seat to plague me, Harry actually put him up to it. As soon as Broken Nose walked through the door, I had him in sight at all times. And I had this in my hand which no one could see." Mister Hickok revealed the Derringer he now had in the palm of his hand, which I didn't know was there.

"Broken Nose walked behind me. I saw him start his draw. I was ready to shoot him between the eyes—to stop his motor functions, of course—when I saw George enter and draw his gun. I relaxed. You know what happened from there on in."

"But what if the General missed?" I asked and was immediately ready to kick myself in the ass.

"He didn't, did he?" Mister Hickok said with his patient smile. "I'm happy to hear George is doing well on the stage. But why not? He's been on the stage all of his life. I hope he is easing up on President Grant. I'd venture to say that once the powers in Washington decide to give up that sham of pretending to be abiding by a treaty and run the Indians out of the Black Hills, the President will send in the troops and drag George back to Washington to stand trial. I'm sure all of those lawyers will be able to find scores of charges."

"General Custer did cut down on this accusations. He no longer blames President Grant personally for the massacre. He now says the President is just stupid for picking such corrupt cronies. He is adamant he could have won the battle if his troops had repeating rifles."

"Can't find fault with that argument."

"Mister Stanley wrote that General Custer had the opportunity to bring along Gatling guns and, if he had them, they would have turned the tide of battle."

"Mister Stanley, as usual, is full of more shit than a fifty-pound turkey vulture. Gatlings are not only clumsy, they are dangerous. Four horses are needed to draw a single gun. And that's on a roadway. They are almost impossible to manhandle through the mountains and forests. Many times I've seen where the horses were unhitched and the troopers drag them over obstacles.

"Gatlings are always malfunctioning. There were invented before the Civil War and hadn't been improved since. I've seen it where bullets sprayed from five to ten barrels at once. A Gatling is essentially a European weapon. Masses of men walking in precision towards them. Indians don't stand around in parade ground order waiting to be shot.

"No, the Gatlings wouldn't have helped. Too cumbersome. Too...ahh...un-American. What would help against the Indian is a lightweight machine-type gun. Something the size of a carbine. It would be a machine rifle. I've been working on the idea for awhile. It could be rigged with an ammunition pan like a Gatling but only fire through one barrel. What has to be solved is to get it to fire repeatedly with one pull of the trigger. I don't know. Maybe the discharged gas from a fired round could somehow advance the next round."

"Is that a drawing of the machine rifle?" I asked, pointing to the small notebook Mister Hickok sketched in when he was by himself.

"No. This is another idea I've been thinking of lately. There are inventors in this country attempting to perfect this object. The Europeans, especially the English, are more advanced. This is a self-propelled vehicle that transports passengers on streets and over roads to their destination. Similar to a steam locomotive but much smaller and it doesn't need tracks. You could call it a horseless stagecoach."

"An engineering professor at State used to preach about them. He was really fanatical. Said horseless coaches were the future. I thought it was something new but he said there was one built more than a hundred years ago. Is that right," I asked as I stripped off the denims and prepared to scrub away the layers of dirt on my body.

"That's a fact. Was just reading about it. A captain in the French army drove a three-wheel steam-powered wagon even before our Revolution. From all accounts, it was practically unmanageable. But he did set a record for two-and-a-half-miles per hour. And he had to stop every couple of hundred feet to steam up."

I was once again impressed by the knowledge of this sensitive, self-educated man. He had a hunger of knowledge and grasped thoughts and concepts quickly. Kit was like that. Very intelligent. Very...But I began thinking of Kit's body and not her brain. My mind drifted but I did manage to listen to Mister Hickok's discourse on the steam carriage. He did go on. And on. And on. Until finally:

"...What surprises me is there isn't more activity being pursued in these United States on the self-propelled vehicle. I've been trying to locate someone who is actually building one. Do you think this professor would know anyone?"

"What? What was that?" I asked, coming out of my thoughts of Kit.

"Did you hear anything I had to say?"

"Yes, Sir. Certainly. But could you just repeat the last part; I had soap in my ear."

"Do you think this professor knows anyone working on such a vehicle?

"I would think so. I could write him and find out."

"Good idea. Please do it. This professor must be considered some sort of visionary."

"Well...more like some sort of crackpot."

"I guess I can understand that," Mister Hickok said. "Now that you are once again clean, would you like to wear one of my silk shirts and ties. It is too warm for a formal coat but you could have one of my brocade vests."

"Yes, Sir," I said and quickly ran to the log house to get the garments. These were items of clothing I had been borrowing when going into town to see Kit. But I'm sure Mister Hickok was aware of that.

I strapped on the old forty-four Colt Dragoon, which was bought cheaply at the local gunsmith's on Mister Hickok's advice. Dragoons had a reputation for being accurate and packing a tremendous wallop. But they were so long and heavy no one wanted to carry them around. And more so with all of the newer lightweight six-shooters on the market.

I wore the Dragoon butt forward on my right side. Mister Hickok wore his two revolvers butt forward and drew them straight up with a backward motion of his hands. He was equally fast and accurate with either hand. Very few shootists possessed his ambidexterity or athletic quickness. Since I had long arms, Mister Hickok suggested cross drawing with my left hand, which was my predominate hand. With practice I was getting faster. And more so when Mister Hickok trimmed down and oiled the holster.

"O.K., empty the cartridges and show me your draw," he said as he rose from his lounging position.

I drew about a half dozen times.

"Not bad, especially considering that weapon. Fortunately, it is so impressive looking, someone will think twice about drawing against it. I certainly hope so. Now let's see how far you progressed. Go over to the clearing," he said as he slid his two Colts inside his belt.

This was a slower draw than if the guns were in their fitted holsters.

"You make the first move," Mister Hickok said as he crossed his arms.

My left hand, which was held in the ready, did not advance more than three inches until Mister Hickok's revolvers were drawn, cocked and aimed; one at the heart, the other between the eyes.

50

I allowed my imagination to take over my senses and tried to feel what those gunfighters felt under the same circumstances in that last fraction of a second of life.

My throat went dry and contracted, preventing me from screaming out please don't shoot; pores opened up and a clammy chill went through my body; my heart lurched, and my anal drew tight.

Looking into Mister Hickok's eyes produced panic. Those warm, smiling eyes, surrounded by the little crinkles of skin in the corners were gone and replaced with blue steel so piercing I could feel the impact of them on my own eyes. I wanted to yell for God. I wanted to yell for my mother. All was gone. All was finished. Life had ended.

"Good. Very good," Mister Hickok said, his revolvers back in his belt. "You're improving. I'm going to have to start worrying about you soon."

Worrying you don't frighten me to death.

"Don't stop to see Kit before finishing the errands," Mister Hickok called out as I rode from camp.

I promised him first things first.

But as I rode down Deadwood Gulch's narrow Main Street, there was Kit yelling and waving frantically from the porch of the whorehouse.

"I'll see you in a little while, Kit. I have to run errands for Mister Hickok. Don't pull a face. Honest I do."

"Please, Franny, this is very important. You have to come here this very minute."

"Don't say very so much. Mister Hickok told me very implicitly I have to…"

"He won't mind. It will be just a minute."

"I don't know…"

"One minute, Franny," she said oh so pathetically, a catch in her throat and a tear in her eye.

"What's wrong, darling?" I asked as I draped my mount's reins over a hitching post and ran towards her.

"You have to see this," she said as she grabbed my hand and dragged me through a parlor of whores to the hallway.

"See what?"

51

"This," Kit said as she kissed me and took my hand, rubbing it over her pussy.

"But the errands..." I said with less conviction and squeezed her firm breast with the other hand. She ran her hand down my body until she grabbed me by my last bit of resistance.

"Come on. Let's have a quickie," she said as she pushed open the door to her room and practically threw me through.

"I can't," I said and gently pushed her away. I showed her the small tablet I pulled from my pocket. "I owe too much."

"Mother!" she screamed.

"What's wrong, Child?" asked Kittie who suddenly materialized. "Did he hurt you? Did he say something to you? I'll cut off his..."

"No, Mother, it isn't anything like that. We can't fuck because he's in the hole, deep in the hole. Show her the tablet, Franny."

"Don't say fuck, Child," Kittie said as she took the tablet. "You two know the agreement." Even she had to raise an eyebrow as she examined the tablet. "For chrissake don't you two do anything besides fuck?"

"Can't we just forget the money now, Mother? I'll do cleaning or something else around here. Please?"

"You can't just give it away. Your college..."

"Please, please. I'll die if we don't...ahh...make love right now. Besides, Franny's in a hurry. He has to run errands for Bill."

"I don't know, Kit. I don't want to set a precedent..."

"I guess I'll just have to go in the parlor and earn some money so I can help Franny pay his..."

"...But on the other hand, I guess there's nothing wrong with breaking the rules now and then. But just one freebee. No more," Kittie said as she left the room.

We were undressed, in bed and making love almost as soon as the door closed.

"Kit, darling, I really hate to make love and run errands. But I..." I started to say as I climbed out of bed and began dressing.

"Your precious errands. You care more about your errands than you do me. Please, just once more."

"We can't. You know what your mother said. Besides, I'll be back soon."

"I guess you don't love me anymore. You're tired of me," Kit said, once again a catch in her throat and a tear in her eye.

"Don't talk so silly, darling. I love you very much. But I have to…" I stopped. I couldn't bear seeing Kit unhappy, even knowing she was faking. "Well, just once more," I said as I again removed my shirt—Mister Hickok's shirt—and jumped in bed with Kit, who was again all smiles as she cuddled up. "Remember this is it. I have to…I have to…I have to…" Then I forgot what I was suppose to remember.

"I don't know how you two can do it so often," Kittie yelled through the door. "But don't forget, young man, you had your freebee. You're back on the book now."

"You are punctual," Mister Roche," said Agnes Hickok as she consulted the small gold watch pinned to her lapel. "Sit here," she added, patting the other side of the sofa in the new Deadwood Hotel.

If I was punctual it was because Mister Hickok knew I couldn't get past Kit and calculated in that time.

"From your smile, I would say you just concluded giving that lovely young girl her…lessons. A giggle.

"Yes, as a matter of fact. I reviewed her homework. This week it is the classics and chemistry."

"I wouldn't know about the classics but I can certainly see the chemistry. I believe you two are deeply in love, aren't you?"

"Well…I…ahh…don't…"

"And I know she is not a child as her mother pretends. I have a daughter too. She would still be twelve if I could help it. Tell me, now, how old is she really?"

"…Ahh…Kit's seventeen. But don't tell anyone. Her mother doesn't want her age known."

"I thought as much. Sixteen or seventeen. A grown woman. I was married when I was sixteen. She is a lovely young woman. So pretty and such an attractive body. You are a fortunate young man to have a woman like her.

"Yes, I know," I said and realized just how fortunate I was.

53

"James thinks a lot of her. That is understandable. How is my James? I can picture him now," she said closing her eyes. "He is perspired and coated with dirt from his hard labor at the claim." She opened her eyes and rolled them upward.

"That's possible. The last time I saw him he was ready to start construction of a new sluice."

"Don't fib. I know my James. He is resting now so he can sneak into town later to play poker. The card table is his real claim for gold. I can tell you are the one who is doing the work."

She took by hands and felt the calluses. She ran her hands up my arm, squeezing forearms and biceps. "You are ready for the trapeze. If you decide to join the circus, come and see me. You and your lady. You two would be natural performers. I'm sure you are already great performers." A leer and a giggle.

"Mister Hickok told me to give you this note," I quickly said, trying to change the subject. I was somewhat embarrassed but I had learned this was Agnes Hickok's direct European manner.

"Thank you," she said, sticking the envelope in the small sack next to her. "I will read it later. I know it won't say anything. I will leave and allow James to enjoy himself."

"Missus Hickok, I know he loves you very much. He says so…"

"I believe that. And I believe he will come back to me. But I know I can not compete with Deadwood Gulch. It offers what he seeks and can no longer find. It is not the gold, it is not the cards, it is not even the whores. It is his last chance to again capture his youth. James is thirty-nine—much younger than myself—and he will be forty soon. This is on his mind very much; the thought of becoming forty years old. It has produced a melancholia. He feels his life is in a crisis, a middle of life crisis. He needs this last frontier to get him across this plateau. This god-forsaken, hellhole of a town is reminiscent of Abilene when he was marshal. To him Deadwood is his last chance to live wild and free. I'm sorry, Mister Roche, to bore you with this…"

"No, no, not at all. This is more insight into Mister Hickok and will help with the record I am attempting to piece together. He is the most fascinating…"

54

"Yes, I know. And you love him very much too. Like a father. And you know he thinks so much of you."

Now I was really embarrassed.

"You American men always hide your love for other men," she said and gently caressed my cheek. "And I'm not talking about sodomites but real men."

I mumbled and looked across the room.

"You tell James I departed on the afternoon stagecoach. Tell him when he is ready to return I'll be waiting for him. And please look after him. Don't allow him to get into danger."

For the first time, Missus Hickok lost her gaiety and smile. There were tears in her eyes. And not Kit tears.

"Don't leave. I can go back to camp and talk to Mister Hickok. Maybe if he knows..."

"Please, my mind is made up. I can't stay here any longer. I still can't sleep through the night thinking that evil little man might have murdered him minutes before I arrived. It brought back the emotions and pain I endured after my first husband died a violent death. William Lake Thatcher, another good man in his way," she said with a sad smile.

"Billy dropped the Thatcher because it was too long for advertising. He was a circus clown when I met him but in a few years we had our own show. I'll never forget his death. It was in August of Sixty-nine while we were in Granby, Missouri, when poor Billy was senselessly killed by Jake Killian, a local desperado."

I knew this. I also knew that in August of Seventy-One, when Agnes Lake brought her circus to Hays City, Marshal Hickok waxed eloquently before town council to reconsider its decision to charge the circus a special tax (a greed-motivated tax). Council, of course, did reconsider. But when Mister Hickok made an offer, who could refuse?

Missus Hickok stood up. She was a small woman and had a firm and attractively-shaped body for a woman so old. She was fifty.

"I'll be leaving now, Mister Roche. Maybe if James strikes gold or no one will play cards with him anymore, he'll be ready to come back to me and perform in the circus. He'd be a wonderful act; even a bigger draw than Buffalo Bill Cody. It is a pity he had such bad experiences in show business. You, of course, know he tried his own Wild West show in Buffalo, New York, and was on the stage with Colonel Cody. He considered both disasters. But James is essentially a private man and doesn't enjoy performing an act in front of people."

Missus Hickok took my arm and led me to the registration desk where two large suitcases were waiting. She concluded her business with the clerk and effortlessly picked up the suitcases.

"Please allow me to carry them."

If you wish, Mister Roche. They really aren't heavy. But I guess it wouldn't look proper for us to walk down the street with a small woman carrying suitcases while a big strong man has his hands in his pockets."

Actually I didn't think anyone in this town would think it improper for a woman to carry suitcases, or anything else for that matter. But she was so small and the suitcases were so big. As I lifted the suitcases, I thought my ballocks would drop to the floor. They were that heavy. By the time we walked to the stage depot, I had the red staggers.

As I set down the suitcases, a prospector—dirty, bearded and three sheets to the wind—approached Missus Hickok.

"What whorehouse are you with, chicken? I got a full poke of gold and an itch to fuck. Just lead the way."

Missus Hickok led, all right, with a right cross that caught the amorous prospector on the chin. The punch sent him back several feet to the wall of the depot, which he hit and then slid down into a heap.

It became apparent why Mister Hickok did not want to rile this woman. The stage driver, who was handing luggage to the shotgun rider on top of the coach, looked on in awe.

"Don't stand there like a tableau, load my suitcases. I am anxious to leave this pit of putrefaction. It is a disgrace when a helpless woman must be accosted by brutish men."

The "brute" was still out cold.

"Yes, Ma'am, right away," the driver said as he grabbed the handle of one of the suitcases and lifted it several inches. With pain in his eyes, he puffed out, "Lend a hand, young man."

Before I could do that, Missus Custer took the suitcase from the driver and tossed it up to the shotgun rider. He was almost knocked off the top of the stagecoach as he caught it. She grabbed the other suitcase and tossed that up too. The shotgun rider backed up and let it bounce on the stagecoach roof.

"Tell my James I love him," Missus Hickok said and hugged me. "And take care of him, please. Here, this is for you and your woman."

I protested payment but she forced it into my hand. I was relieved to see it wasn't money but two complimentary tickets to the Lake Circus. They were signed by James A. Bailey.

The stage driver offered Missus Hickok an arm as she turned to enter the stagecoach. Not necessary. She swung through the door opening as if it were a trapeze.

"And tell James to stay away from the whores," were her last words as the six snorting stagecoach steeds galloped away, causing pedestrians to scatter for their lives.

I was amused and somewhat honored that she thought I could take care of her James. She never called him Bill. But then it wasn't his Christian name and her first husband was named William.

I did not have time to ponder on this thought. I had to see General Custer at the Langrishe Theatre. The Langrishe until recently had been the Bella Union. Jack Langrishe, the Black Hill's foremost comedian, who also considered himself an impresario, was leasing the log building until his own theatre was completed. The theatre had the usual variety acts, a dance hall and gambling games. General Custer's act was, as Mister Langrishe called it, the crown jewel in a tiara of rhinestones.

The Langrishe was located next to the No. 10, which could get boisterous at times. And at these times General Custer got very angry because the noise interfered with his presentation. So angry at times that he went over and threatened to shoot the next man who raised his voice. Fortunately, the neighbor on the theatre's other flank was quiet. This was a lunch counter modestly named "Crumbs of Comfort Along the Crack in the Wall."

Even before entering the theatre, I could hear the General haranguing Jack Langrishe. The General seemed to enjoy haranguing simply for the sake of haranguing.

This time he was threatening to take his act to the Gem Variety Theatre and Dancehall, which featured a girlie show of thirty dancers. This establishment had the reputation of anything goes. Quite a comment in a wide-open town like Deadwood.

"General! Are you telling me you would actually take your high moral quality performance—a very crucial piece of history and Americana, which every man, woman and child should experience—to that glorified whorehouse?" Mister Langrishe turned to me and winked.

"If you don't believe me, ask you trusted associate here. A fine young man. A college graduate from the East. A man untainted by the wickedness and wiles of the West. A man I even trust to count the house receipts. And that, Sir, is an honor afforded very few men. I defer to young Mister Roche. You tell General Custer why he shouldn't go to the Gem."

I really didn't want to be caught in the middle. The General could be unreasonable at times, to put it mildly. He was downright outrageously ridiculous in his sensitivities for the feelings of others. He was a man that could be admired. A man that could be respected. A man that could be trusted. He was not, however, a man that could be liked. His troopers didn't name him Hard Ass and Iron Butt as compliments.

But, as I looked at him now, attired for his performance in the clothing he wore at the Little Big Horn, I got a catch in my throat and a slight tingle through my limbs for just being close to this controversial and colorful personage.

He wore blue trousers with a gold stripe running down the leg, deeply polished black knee-high boots, a fringed buckskin jacket over a white silk shirt and an immaculate white soft Stetson. Around his neck was a kerchief, red above, blue below, with a brace of crossed sabers on the two dangling ties; the same pattern as his personal flag. Around his waist was a saber in a polished brass holster that gleamed like gold.

The General hadn't worn the saber at the Little Big Horn. For some reason, yet to be satisfactory explained, the Seventh's

58

sabers were packed in boxes and left at the Powder River depot. I also suspected this was not the outfit worn on that tragic day. But who gave a rat's ass? The General looked spectacular—the way everyone would want to believe he looked that day.

And he looked more dashing than ever. His golden hair was once again shoulder length. His moustache long and full. And once again there was the small triangular beard under his lower lip to the top of his chin.

But I had to agree with Mister Langrishe; it would be a tactical error to move to the Gem. Mister Langrishe gave General Custer the entire theatre for his presentation. The bar was closed; the gambling tables shut down, the variety acts not allowed to practice and drunks kept out.

Also, as he said, Mister Langrishe, under the watchful eye of him and the General allowed me to take in the gate and split the proceeds. I had no doubt that the low lives at the Gem would not only steal the money but General Custer's saber as well.

I had no idea why the General wanted to go to the Gem. It couldn't have been for the thirty dancers. Actually, dancing was a liberal assessment of what these women performed on the stage. Old Peg Leg Johnny, yet another splash on the tapestry of local color, had more grace staggering out of a saloon. And their single forte, fucking, was not needed even by a man with such a voracious sexual appetite. No, the General didn't need the professionals. He had many amateurs waiting in the wings. Mister Langrishe was advertising the General's lecture in newspapers throughout the territory, and this attracted many young women. Single, attractive, young women who wanted a piece of historic ass. The General tried not to disappoint his admirers.

"Mister Langrishe is correct. The Gem is no place for your...ahh...talent and high standards. You are a part of history and to have to..."

"What? You traitor. You're siding against me? Am I clasping another Major Reno to my bosom? And what is this nonsense that I have to..."

"I was trying to say that you have to share your experiences with all classes of people. Not just..."

"Whores," Mister Langrishe injected. "Yes, you have to share with those young, nubile, pulchritudinous, pure women who come—yes, come—to sit at the feet of this country's finest hero. Many of who are college cooperative students who will return to campus with the fruits of General Custer's tree. His manhood, his vitality. His essence. Would you trade this for those whores at the Gem? Because that is what you would have to do. You know those fine young women would not set a foot in that affront to Sodom and Gomorrah."

"Well...humm...you may have a point there. Yes, I must share. But there is no excusing the noise from the Number Ten. Just when I am at some important junction in my narrative, some yahoo has to spew forth with vulgarities of the coarsest nature. Many of the young women are mortified by this language; as they have informed me later that night."

"General, that shouldn't be a problem any longer. I just escorted Missus Hickok to the stagecoach," I said. "She is now on her way back to the circus. Mister Hickok is free to come to the Number Ten at all hours. I'm sure he'd be only too happy to play cards during the performance."

"About time that old harpy left. Yes, Bill certainly would keep those yahoos and bozos quiet. But what about..." Before General Custer could come up with another complaint, Mister Langrishe made his escape. The General stared at the open door and cursed softly under his breath.

"Perhaps Jack is right. All of those nubile and pulchritudinous..." the General interrupted himself to flash a lustful leer at two young women fitting this description standing outside and giggling as they waved to him.

"Francis Scott. Those young women outside. I know they are here for my performance. Why don't you inquire as to their names and make a schedule to when they can meet me in private. Be generous. Give each at least twenty minutes."

"Sir, as we discussed previously, my duties do not extend to being a procurer. But you really don't need a roster, they seem more than willing to wait their turn..." Seeing General Custer's eyes narrow and nares flare, I shot an arrow—perhaps bad choice of words—at his only soft spot. "How is Missus Custer?

Only this morning Mister Hickok again told me what a lovely, intelligent, woman she is. The prettiest girl in…"

"Yes, dear, dear Elizabeth. The most wonderful wife a man could have. I just received a message from her. No good news but then no worse news. President Grant is still angry at the truths I speak. My dear Libbie. I miss her so. Napoleon at least had his Josephine at Saint Helena. What do I have?"

For one thing, all of those nubile and pulchritudinous young women. The Napoleon-Josephine-Saint Helena-Exile theme was a frequent subject for General Custer. But from what Mister Hickok, Mister Stanley and Harry Young said he was damn lucky to have his Saint Helena in the Black Hills. The federal government still hadn't made a move. There was no doubt that the government would claim it, despite any previous treaty with the Indians. The only question was when?

Until that time, General Custer was safe. Or as safe as anyone could be in the Black Hills. President Grant could not send in the troops—no doubt the Fifth Cavalry—until he made a decision. And the President was not the most decisive decision-maker to grace the White House. He preferred to let things ride in hope they would solve themselves.

Mister Hickok thought that while Libbie might not be able to change the President's mind about her husband, she probably charmed him enough to even delay further his delaying tactics. There was talk that the Army would enter the Black Hills if the Indians attacked any of the white settlements. That was plain bunk. The Indian population had declined considerably. They were paying dearly for their victory at the Little Big Horn. Those who were not dead were fleeing to Canada, just a few steps ahead of the Army. Crazy Horse was believed to be there.

"What, what do I have?" the General continued morosely. He brightened up quickly when he saw several more female admirers standing outside. These women seemed to come in groups.

"Mister Hickok sent this note."

General Custer took the note, read it quickly and placed it on top of Missus Custer's letter.

"Poor Bill's complaining about the hardships at our claim. He doesn't know yet that Agnes left, huh? I shouldn't keep the good news from him too long. I'll dispatch a runner." He called over to the barroom in the next room for an old Army veteran who did odd jobs for him. The veteran stood at attention as General Custer gave his instructions. The General returned the veteran's salute as he left.

"And how is our claim progressing?"

I explained how "we" were tunneling into the hillside, sinking a shaft into the ground, running a sluice on the streamlet and cracking rocks.

"Yes. It is hard work. I was just telling Elizabeth that. Even more so since that goddamn idiot Colorado Charlie staked out the most barren claim in the Hills. When I led my military expedition in the summer of Seventy-four, I saw gold every place I pissed."

General Custer's expedition into the Black Hills wasn't some half-assed look here and there. It was a well equipped, rounded out, full exploratory effort.

There were a thousand men under the General including ten companies of the Seventh; one each of the Twentieth and Seventeenth Infantry; one hundred Indian scouts from the Rees, Santees and Sioux; guides, interpreters and teamsters. He even had artillery. The expedition drove one hundred and ten wagons, rode one thousand cavalry horses and drove three hundred head of cattle for slaughter.

There were also scientific men including geologists, naturalists, medical officers, and botanists. There were also a good number of photographers and correspondents. The least conspicuous members of this group were two practical miners. The most conspicuous, a full military band.

When the General gave his report on the Black Hills, he dwelt at length at their beauty. There was even a passage about the flowers being so abundant in one valley that his soldiers bedecked their horses and selves with them and stopped to listen to the music of the band.

Somewhere near the end of the report, almost as an afterthought, he disclosed gold was found in French Creek, the heart of the Hills.

The mention of gold was not lost on anyone. The news quickly reached the East, and every other point of the compass. The rush was on. Soon the Army had to protect the white settlers who didn't belong there and keep out the Indians who did.

"The curse of leadership is I have to do everything myself. I'll have to visit the camp and show you how to find gold."

"Excellent idea, General. The sun comes up early here. You could come out four-thirty or five tomorrow morning and we could begin."

"Maybe not that early and maybe not tomorrow but sometime when I can get away from my responsibilities. But right now I have to rest before my performance." He beckoned with a leer and movement of his head to two of his responsibilities who were slowly making their way towards him. Both very nubile, both very pulchritudinous, both very smiling.

"Isn't it time to give Kit her lessons," he said with a leer and wiggle of his eyebrows. "She's developed into a lovely young woman. But no surprise considering her parents. I will have to take her riding soon. Don't look at me that way. I've been taking her riding since she was a little girl. I have my obligations. I'm her godfather, you know."

"No, I didn't know. Then who is her…"

"Do I have to tell you a second time to see Kit," he said as he allowed the two young women to each take an arm and led them to his dressing room.

"No, Sir," I snapped and was out the door and on my way. So I'll owe Mister Hickok more money. What the hell. I almost knocked over Harry Young who was standing outside the No. 10 Ten.

"On your way to see Kit?" he yelled to my vanishing back.

The claim camp was quiet early Sunday morning as Kit and I rode in on the bare back of Ulysses, the big Percheron that was once a circus performer. Mister Langrishe had bought Ulysses with the idea he would ride him as part of his act. But he wisely decided to stick to his wit instead of his horsemanship.

Ulysses did little work besides pulling a wagon now and then and was only too happy when I took him out for exercise. Besides being huge, he was about eighteen hands and two thousand pounds, he was extremely intelligent. He performed on voice command; not only in English but several European languages. (Missus Hickok demonstrated this.) But he had his independent side. If he didn't like something he'd let you know.

Right now, Ulysses was being very sweet. He had only been to the camp once before but he found his way without any help. This was fortunate because it gave Kit and I more time to fool around.

Ulysses stopped. This meant we had arrived. As soon as we dismounted, Ulysses lowered his head and nodded towards the feed bag. I didn't bother to fasten it but just held the canvas bag of grain out to him. I loved all horses but I loved big horses and, almost as much, mules a little more.

Even as a little kid I knew I would someday be in the West. I learned to ride about the same time I could walk. And not at a riding academy or anything like that. First it was mules from the anthracite mines back in Wilkes-Barre. My father would take me to the mule stable after Mass on Sunday and I would ride until it was time for dinner. That was before he was killed in a cave-in. Then it was draught horses from the barns of the agricultural school at State. Every male student was required to work ten hours a week on the school farm, in the garden, or at the barn. I took care of the wagon and plow horses, mostly Belgians and Clydesdales.

"Oh what a beautiful morning," Kit said as she hugged me. "Pay attention to me. I swear you love Ulysses more than you love me." She took a handful of mane and playfully tugged on it. Ulysses turned an eye to her and winked. I swear.

Yes, it was beautiful. And the beauty of nature was emphasized by the quiet; something very seldom experienced in mining country. The miners and prospectors were still drinking or sleeping it off in town. Mister Hickok was, no doubt, fast asleep at Kittie's after a hard night at the poker table. General

Custer was probably having a well-deserved rest after satisfying his group of admirers, or, as Kit called them, groupers.

Colorado Charlie was somewhere in the Black Hills seeking a more productive claim. Or so he said he would be. More than likely he was passed out on the floor of some whorehouse. General Custer had chewed out his ass so badly for staking this claim that Charlie said he wouldn't come back until he redeemed his reputation as a prospector. General Custer had drawn a crude sketch of where he thought he might have seen gold gleaming in the stream or on rock surfaces. He wasn't really sure. It had been two years ago. Charlie said if it were there he would find it.

Kit took a blanket from the tent, shook it furiously, then spread it near the streamlet on soft fern still damp with dew. She sat down, stretched out her arms and beckoned. I went to her arms and squeezed her until she groaned. She held my hand and shook her head as I began unbuttoning her dress.

Please, let's just hug and kiss," and perhaps sensing my disappointment and disbelief, added, "It's that period of the month. You should be thankful."

I was thankful for everything. Especially thankful for having Kit in my arms. I held her gently and kissed her. I kissed her lips, kissed her cheeks, kissed her eyes, kissed her ears, kissed her forehead, kissed her neck.

"That's so nice. So nice," Kit whispered as she softly moaned.

Time may have passed. Maybe it didn't. I had no idea. I was lost in Kit.

Suddenly, I sat up quietly and placed my hand over Kit's mouth. Something or someone was out there. I slowly got to my feet, strapped on the Dragoon and walked away from Kit, motioning her not to move.

A rifle cracked. A projectile passed so close to my right ear I could feel the wake. I was ready to dive but then remembered how General Custer had deviled his brother Boston. Another crack. This time my left ear. No doubt about it. The General. If someone wanted to hit me, he would have done it by now. This could be a great opportunity to impress Kit.

"Come on down, you yahoo. I'm not afraid. I'll fight you with my bare hands. I'll fight you with one hand behind my back."

"Franny! Get down, please," Kit pleaded.

Another crack of the rifle. This time a small chunk of earth exploded between my feet. Maybe I shouldn't tempt the General so much. Kit ran at me and executed a textbook-perfect flying block that caught me in the chest. We hit the ground as puffs of dirt exploded around us. Now more shooting and the pounding of hoofs.

A band of riders, miners and cowboys, led by General Custer, galloped past and up the hill in the direction of the firing. Mister Hickok was in the rear. He pulled up his horse and dismounted.

"Thank God you young ones are alive," he said and hugged Kit. "We've been pursuing that war party since daybreak. They attacked a camp outside of Deadwood. Miners slept through it. Drunk. Just as well, no one got killed. George thinks they might have came after him. Who knows? We heard gunfire from this direction. I knew you two were here. I thought...I thought..." Mister Hickok wiped his eye and gave Kit another hug. He reached over and gave me a playful slap on the cheek. Really not that playful.

"Franny was so brave," Kit said and told him of my misguided bravado.

He looked at me and raised an eyebrow. "It seems to me I heard that story before. Nevertheless, you performed a brave deed. You may have confused them or they would have charged in and killed both of you." He hugged Kit again and gave me another not so playful slap.

"I don't want you to get the wrong idea, Sir, but I thought..."

General Custer rode up. "They're on the run. I haven't a chance of catching them," he yelled as he alighted from Comanche. Among the many charges against him was that he stole Comanche. He always claimed the horse was the personal property of Myles Keogh and, in his dying breath, that brave Irishman passed Comanche onto him.

"He's tired," General Custer said as he ran a hand over Comanche's flank. "The scar is holding but I don't believe he should be rode again, never. He's too much a part of history." He rubbed his head against Comanche's. "You'll live the rest of your life in pasture."

"Uncle George, wait until I tell you what Franny did," Kit said and did.

General Custer looked at me, arched an eyebrow and turned to Mister Hickok. "Why does that sound so familiar?"

"We better get back to town," Mister Hickok said, "and make sure those drunks don't start shooting at each other for Indians." He climbed into his saddle and held out an arm. Kit grabbed it and swung gracefully behind him.

General Custer stripped his tack from Comanche, fashioned a loose rope halter for him and handed me the bitter end.

"Allow him to rest at least an hour before you walk him back to town. Where's your mount?"

I managed to keep a straight face as I pointed to the little grove where Ulysses was hidden.

"By the Eternal," he shouted. "You expect me to ride that goddamn beer wagon plug?"

"Please, Sir. Ulysses is very sensitive. He's…"

"Ulysses? The same name as that man in the White House who wants to put me before a firing squad? Do you think I'm going to ride him?"

Mister Hickok and Kit were laughing so hard they almost fell off their horse.

"George, don't be so disrespectful of that fine animal. Agnes fell in love with that horse and wanted to take him back to the circus. But Jack wouldn't sell him."

"Well, I don't know," General Custer said, giving a wary eye to Ulysses, who returned the gesture.

"Come on, George. He's a Percheron, a noble beast. The breed was the mount of choice for armored knights during the Middle Ages. They have considerable stamina and are good trotters."

Ulysses ears perked up.

"What the hell," General Custer said, grabbing Ulysses' mane and swinging on his back; an impressive feat of horsemanship in itself, more so considering he was holding his saddlebags and our picnic basket in his other hand. "Move out," he said, spurring on Ulysses with his heels. Ulysses did not move.

"You have to speak to him, Sir. You have to call him by his name or he won't do anything," I said and winked at Mister Hickok and Kit.

"You expect me to say that name? Never." General Custer said, spurring on Ulysses even more vigorously. He got tired before Ulysses even moved an inch.

"Do I really have to call him by his name?"

"No, Sir. I could ride him and you could walk Comanche, if you prefer." Again, another wink at Mister Custer and Kit, who were again almost falling off their horse. But I was even beginning to feel pity for General Custer. I reached up and patted Ulysses on the side of his head. "Ulysses, take General Custer back to the stable." Ulysses nodded, I swear, and started walking towards town.

"We can't leave Franny here with Indians around," Kit said.

"Don't worry, Dear," General Custer said, "the Indians are probably in Wyoming by now. Besides, the riders will be passing this way soon. And don't forget your beau can frighten away Indians just yelling at them. Har, har."

"Don't worry, Kit. I'll see you in town soon. We can eat our picnic lunch then," I yelled after them. General Custer was holding the basket and passing out food to the others as he held a big fried chicken leg in his mouth.

I took the halter off Comanche. He went to the streamlet and began drinking. As I kept a guard on him so he wouldn't drink too much, I noticed a glitter in the water where the gravel appeared to be disturbed. Could this be where the two shots that whizzed by my head landed? I didn't want to get excited because I knew it could be pyrite, quartz, or even crystal.

I brushed the surface gravel aside gently and saw more glittering. Now I was getting excited. I filled a small poke with samples the size of prairie hen eggs. There appeared to be several traces of minerals in the samples and they had considerable weight.

I wasn't sure it was gold but I wasn't sure it wasn't. For the first time I wished Charlie were here. Maybe he couldn't find gold but he could identify it. I doubted very much if Mister Hickok or General Custer could recognize traces of gold embedded in another mineral. Maybe I should have taken another geology course.

I brushed down Comanche, then talked and played with him until I was certain he was rested. I gently mounted his bare back and softly prodded him with my knees.

"Don't worry, Boy, I won't hurt you. I'm just going to ride you a stretch up the trail. I want to look back when I'm an old man and say I was the last man to ride the famous Comanche.

"Bill, I gotta talk to you. Bill, we got to talk. We could swap…" Colorado Charlie stopped. He looked suspiciously at the other card players at the table. He had no need worrying about them listening to him. They were all staring intently at their cards.

Harry Young set a mug of beer in front of me. I sprinkled in grains of salt from the big glass shaker. White streams streaked to the bottom of the mug and then bubbled up. I needed the beer and I needed the salt. It was more than one hundred degrees in the sun and not a wisp of wind was blowing. I'd been running all day. Some errands for Mister Hickok, some for General Custer and some for Mister Stanley, who may have been a condescending ass but at least paid well. I also dispatched several stories back East. I wanted to see Kit but first I had to talk to Mister Hickok. But, unlike Charlie, I knew better than to disturb him at cards, especially since he was losing. Mister Hickok was not a happy loser.

"Come on, Bill, come on outside. I gotta talk to you," Charlie persisted as he grabbed Mister Hickok by the arm and almost tipped him off his stool.

"Charlie, let go of me. This is a big hand…"

"This is important. It's about…" again looking around suspiciously.

"Could we play cards here?" snapped Jerry Lewis, who was also losing.

"It's about the claim, Bill. We got a chance to get a sure thing. Those jaspers..."

"I'll see your wager and double it, Captain."

"Those jaspers on top of the mountain...they want to...but they don't know...goddamn't, Bill, we got to talk. We have the opportunity..."

Mister Hickok stared intently at his cards. "Is it about the claim, Charlie?" he asked without looking up.

"That's what I'm trying to tell you..."

"Do what has to be done. Don't bother me. I have important work at this table."

"It'll make us rich, Bill, rich," Charlie said as he ran to the door,

I wasn't paying much attention to Charlie, he was always excited, but watching the game, as everyone else was doing. It was a big game. There were eight players at the table, including two big cattlemen, a scion of a wealthy New England family, and one of the major stockholders in the Homestake Mine. The center of the table was piled with gold and silver coins and large denomination greenback notes, along with small pokes of dust and nuggets.

Mister Hickok motioned to me with his eyes. I knew what he wanted; the money I carried for him that he told me never give to him if he asked for it at the card table.

"Hand it over. It's a sure thing."

"But..." I performed my obligatory knee bend protest and handed the wad to Mister Hickok.

The stakes went even higher and Mister Hickok was short on the final raise. Anyone would have given him credit; he was an honest player and had a reputation for paying his debts. But he would sooner fold than ask a favor. That was his code.

In my best thespian endeavor—one does not spend all that time around General Custer without learning dramatics—I tossed the small poke of ore into the pot. "This will more than cover it, gentlemen."

Everyone agreed.

70

"I don't care what's in the poke, ore, dust, or pebbles," said the man from the Homestake, "I accept it as your bet."

"Thank you. But I insist everyone take a look," Mister Hickok said as he dumped the contents on the table. Glittering small rough stones scattered.

The Homestead man quickly gathered them in a pile and pushed it in front of Mister Hickok. "This isn't necessary," he said as he spread his cards on the table. "But, Mister Hickok, I feel this hand is a winner. Just as the Homestake Mine is a winner. Only I'm not willing to bet it."

His hand, after discarding the two extra cards in this game of Seven Up, was a full house; three kings over a pair of jacks.

"He should have bet the Homestake," Harry Young whispered.

As it came their turn, the other players quietly placed their cards in front of them, face down. The last player was Mister Hickok and he kept staring at his closely grouped cards. The Great Stone Face showed more expression. There wasn't a sound in the crowded saloon. Even the consumptive Pennsylvania artist stopped coughing and the asthmatic New York photographer stopped wheezing.

Finally.

"Three bullets and a pair of eights. This was the hand I was seeking when that son-of-a-bitch..." Mister Hickok snapped his fingers and looked at me.

"Dirty Jack McCall."

"...Tried to shoot me."

A flash of powder brightened the saloon at the New York photographer took his picture. The Pennsylvania artist began frantically working at his easel. Respectively, they resumed wheezing and coughing.

The saloon crowd whooped.

"Drinks are on me, gentlemen," Mister Hickok announced, majestically waving his arm to the bar.

The players congratulated Mister Hickok on what was the highest stake game ever played in Deadwood Gulch.

"Interesting specimens of ore, young man," said the Homestake man as he picked up a sample and examined it closely. "May I inquire where you obtained them?"

We both looked at Mister Hickok, who nodded as he gathered in the pot.

"At our claim, Sir."

"I thought as much. Not a high grade ore. Not enough content to interest a big mining operation. And please, gentlemen, I am not saying this as a bargaining ploy."

I nodded. Mister Hickok appeared oblivious to the observations as he stacked dust in one pile, nuggets in another, coin in another, and the greenbacks in yet another.

"A couple of men could earn decent money if they put in some hard work. Not the best claim in the Black Hills but certainly better than most. I'm sure you are aware of that."

"Yes, Sir. Miss Kittie, Kit and I spoke to several assayers. But you know how they are. Some you can trust. Some you can't. We sent a sample by stage to the School of Mines and the evaluation just came back. It basically said what you said. But I do value your opinion."

"Thank you. I would offer an advancement of capital against returns, but I think Mister Hickok has all the capital he needs now. Isn't that right, Mister Hickok?"

"What?" Mister Hickok asked as he arranged the piles of mineral, coin and paper into smaller divisions. "Oh, yes, the claim. Very good, Francis Scott. I'm happy but I want to relish this for just a little longer." He began subdividing the divided piles.

"We got it, Bill, we got it," Colorado Charlie shouted as he knocked over the tripod of the photographer and the easel of the artist in his rush to the card table, waving a piece of paper.

Mister Hickok ignored Charlie as he made neater piles and asked me for a tablet and pen.

"Got what?" I asked since everyone else was also ignoring him.

"The claim on the mountain. I traded our worthless claim for the whole top of the mountain."

At last Mister Hickok's attention was aroused.

"You did what?"

Charlie repeated his story. This time elaborating with cliché and clinched teeth. Mister Hickok sat in stunned silence. In fact, the entire saloon population stood or sat in stunned silence.

"Charlie, I've known you too long to shoot you, but goddamn't do you have any idea what you did? You gave away a good claim. Look at this," Mister Hickok said, handing him one of the samples from the poke.

Charlie examined it and sneered. "Junk. Not worth the sweat of sticking a shovel in the ground." He tossed the sample away. It landed in a spittoon

The Homestake man frowned but kept his opinion to himself. Harry Young rolled his eyes upward. The crowd wisely did not get between old friends.

"The first time I have ever struck gold. I think of the hard work and long hours I put into this enterprise. Right, Francis Scott?"

"Absolutely."

"I could have wrote to Agnes that I was actually mining. My dear mother would have been relieved to learn her son no longer had to gamble or risk his life as a lawman. I could have sent them photographs. Right?" he said to the New York photographer.

Wheeze. "Absolutely." Wheeze.

"What if it isn't the best claim in the Black Hills? That's not the point. It would set their minds at ease. They wouldn't have to worry. And you gave it away. "I don't…"

"Calm down, pardner. Calm down. You have a real claim now. A bonanza. You think I'm stupid? I know what I'm doing. Just wait until you see this claim. Your eyes will pop out."

After a couple of minutes of persuasion, Mister Hickok agreed to look at the traded claim. He deposited his winnings in the No. 10's safe and we went to the livery stable to get our horses. The new claim was beyond the old claim. Mister Hickok cursed softly all the way.

"Looky, looky, didn't I tell you," Charlie said as he removed a blanket from an outcrop. "Almost pure gold. That's the highest quality ore I ever seen."

A circle about two feet in diameter glistened with gold. Mister Hickok ran his hand over the surface.

"And look at this one over here," Charlie said, practically dragging Mister Hickok to another outcrop also covered with a blanket. When the blanket was removed, an even larger circle of gold glistened. Mister Hickok examined it closely. He even slipped on his seldom seen spectacles.

"Didn't I tell you, Bill? Didn't I tell you? Did you ever see anything like this in your life? Huh? Huh?"

"Unfortunately, yes, Charlie," Mister Hickok said as he removed his spectacles, placed them in their case and placed the case in his shirt pocket. "The claim's been salted. Some jasper loaded up a shotgun with a couple of hundred dollars of gold slivers, and standing about here," walking back a couple of feet, "blasted away. Here's the right barrel. Here's the left. The pattern's spread out more on the left because it was further away."

"How could I be so goddamn stupid, Bill? I'm sorry. I must have been in the sun too long. I didn't think. I got greedy when I saw that gold glittering."

"Now, now, don't worry about it, old pard," Mister Hickok said, placing an arm around Charlie's shoulders. "We'll just visit those yahoos and trade back. I don't know, Charlie, my reputation must be wearing out. I never thought I'd live to see the day when someone tried to bamboozle me with a salted claim."

"Bill, they didn't know you were my partner. I handled this all by myself. I wanted you to be proud."

"I have always been proud to have you as my friend. So, those bozos didn't know I was a partner in this claim?"

Mister Hickok was more relieved that his reputation had not been violated than he was angry over the bogus bonanza.

"But, Charlie, after I straighten this out, our claim will have to be worked. And you're going to have to do your share. George, Francis Scott and myself can't do all the work all of the time."

Even though Charlie swore he would work hard every day at the claim, I didn't expect to see him around any more than the

74

Legends of the West. More than likely, Kit and I would do the work.

"What are you poking around for?" Mister Hickok asked. "We have to get back to town so I can settle this misunderstanding."

"I don't know. There are some other deposits here. I'm not sure. Maybe it's…"

"Nothing there, son," Charlie said. "Maybe some worthless traces of minerals. I might have been hoodwinked by those jaspers salting gold but there's nothing else of value in those rocks."

"I'll catch up with you in town, Sir. Might as well chip out this gold before you trade back."

"Good idea. See, Charlie, what a college education does," Mister Hickok said as he and Charlie began riding away

As I chipped off the gold traces, a grayish-colored mineral cropped up. It wasn't silver. I knew that and again regretted not taking another geology course at State. Maybe it isn't anything of value but it was all around. It popped up on every rock I hit. Better be safe and take some samples to town.

I swooped Kit off the porch of the whorehouse, where she was sitting in a rocking chair reading a textbook, and carried her to the middle of the street before she had a chance to arouse me, not the most difficult thing for her to do.

"This is so romantic, Franny," she said, clinging to my neck as I deposited her on the porch of the Deadwood Hotel. "Gee, you're taking me to a hotel."

"Maybe later but right now you have to do a couple of things." I gave her the vial of gold slivers from the salted claim to sell. She was a tough bargainer and would get the top price. I told her to take the pieces of gray mineral to several assayers for their opinion. "Be discreet, don't tell them it's from around here. If they get nosy, tell them a Canadian left a bag of it at the whorehouse."

"It doesn't look like much," Kit said turning over one of the samples in her hand. "I know it isn't silver."

"I even know that. Maybe it isn't anything but there's a whole mountain of it."

She pulled a face and ran off.

I found Mister Hickok and Colorado Charlie standing in front of the Gem. Charlie was laughing so hard there were tears in his eyes and he repeatedly slapped his thigh. Mister Hickok looked his usual nonchalant self.

"I thought those jaspers were going to shit when you told them it was your claim. Hoo, boy. You should have seen them, Francis Scott. Their knees were knocking and their teeth clicking. They handed over our claim so fast I didn't have time to open my mouth. And Bill didn't even have to threaten them. Just said the thought they made a mistake. They nodded their heads so fast I thought they were going to fall off. Hoo, boy."

Just then, General Custer and Kit could be seen running towards us. They were hand in hand and it was difficult to see who was pulling whom.

"Glad we caught you, Bill. Kit couldn't find you at the Number Ten and came to me. Tell him, dear," General Custer said, a big smile on his face and parental arm around Kit.

Kit took Mister Hickok's hand and placed one of the gray streaked samples in his hand.

"What are you two all excited about? Isn't this the rock your beau was chipping away at the salted claim? What am I suppose to look for?

"Look at it closer," she urged.

"Mister Hickok looked around to make sure no one was around, then took out his spectacle case. After a minute: "What's that gray mineral? It isn't silver."

"Tin," the General and Kit yelled. They looked around, and in almost a whisper, "tin."

"So what's the big hubbub," Charlie sneered. "Tin isn't worth a fart in the wind. We're after gold. Not that goddamn…"

"Charlie, button that flap for a minute and let them speak," Mister Hickok said.

"This is high-grade tin. From what Kit told me of what Francis Scott told her, we own the whole mountain. We're rich. We struck the mother lode."

"So what? What can you do with tin?" Charlie again sneered.

"Tinned canisters," General Custer snapped. "The Army has been getting more of its food in tinned canisters. Pioneers value tinned canisters. Everybody will be eating food from tinned canisters. This tin is worth its weight in gold. Tinned canisters are the wave of the future."

The General was about as excited as I've ever seen him. Everyone started to get excited as he explained further the fortune to be made in tinned canisters. Until...

"We traded the claim back for ours," Mister Hickok said softly.

The General did not lose a beat.

"Let's not stand around here. We have to trade back."

"There they are. There's those jaspers," Charlie said, pointing to the two men stepping out of the Gem.

They looked like they were just trying to sneak away when Charlie yelled out. They turned several shades whiter and threw up their hands.

"We're sorry, Mister Hickok. We didn't mean anything. We were just leaving town, if that's agreeable with you?" one of the men said, the other nodded his assent.

"Now hold on, gentlemen, no one's mad at anyone," Mister Hickok said as he smiled and walked towards them, shoving back General Custer and Charlie. "I'm the one who should be apologizing. A deal is a deal and I want to stick by my partner's original deal. Let's just swap claims again and call it quits. You two gentlemen mine that claim with out blessing. All of us here are friends."

They handed the original claim paper to Mister Hickok with thanks and bows. They looked as if the lynching party said it had to cancel the event because a rope couldn't be found. They scurried away, throwing more thanks over their shoulders.

"All of this high finance makes me hungry," Kit said and giggled.

"We'll go to the hotel and have something to eat," I said.

"I'm not hungry for food, stupid. I'm hungry to be fucked. But we'll go to the hotel anyway."

"Kit, you are going to have to start watching your language," Mister Hickok said and tsked-tsked her. "You'll be attending college soon and you know college girls don't talk that way."

THREE

A week later, early afternoon, Main Street, Deadwood Gulch, Dakota Territory.

Mister Hickok squinted down Main Street at the strange caravan approaching. He was dressed in work clothes; denim trousers and shirt, mining boots, and Panama hat. The Panama was now sweat-stained and dirty but it had been almost new when he won it in a poker hand a couple of days ago. Instead of his matched pair of Colts in holsters around his waist, he had his old Smith&Wesson six-shooter tucked in his belt.

Between his gambling at night and work at the claim during the day, Mister Hickok had a busy week. We just arrived in town to get supplies for the camp, some grub and maybe a beer or two. But whatever was traveling up the street was now the main attraction.

"Maybe it's a minstrel show? That one wagon is filled with Negro men and Negro women and children are running alongside."

"No. There's no music. There's no laughter. I feel trouble coming, Son. I feel it deep inside," Mister Hickok said and reached to check for his guns. He grimaced.

"That's the worse kind of scum riding along those wagons. I've seen plenty of those ambushers during the border wars in poor Bleeding Kansas. I didn't think they were around anymore."

About a dozen riders surrounded the four wagons. All were dirty, all were mean looking and all were heavily armed. In addition to hand guns that seemed to be strapped everyplace on their bodies, each carried a new repeating rifle.

Four Negro men sat in the lead open wagon. Behind it was a wagon stacked high with something I couldn't identify at that distance. In the rear were two Conestoga wagons.

"Buffalo hides," Mister Hickok said. The odor growing stronger as the wagons came closer. "There's not enough buffalo left for the Indian and these yahoos killed off all of these animals for hides."

As the wagons drew closer, it was apparent that the four Negro men weren't as much sitting in the wagon as being tied to it. A thick rope was strung from neck to neck. And now the sobs and pleading of the women could be heard.

Mister Hickok took a step towards the caravan but stopped when the marshal—a former deputy of Mister Hickok's who was offered the job after Mister Hickok refused it several times—walked in the middle of the street and raised his hand to halt the strange procession.

The lead rider, the ugliest and meanest-looking one of all, waved his arm to stop the wagons and rode up to the marshal.

"Just the man I'm looking for. I've got a claim around here and you could tell me where to find it. I need supplies and want to know where the biggest livery is. You can direct me to both. Maybe you should ride around to show me. And you can tell me where my pardners are. You should know them. Tim Brady and Johnny Varnes and the Montana boys. I haven't time to waste so don't just stand there."

"Hold on there, stranger. I'm not being paid to welcome you to town or act as your guide," the marshal said as he looked from one rider to another. "I'm paid to keep the peace and enforce the law. I don't like what I see here. You can start answering some questions. Why are these Blacks bound up like turkeys? If they committed a crime, the law, not you, will handle them. If not, I want them released. Now!"

"Sure they committed a crime, marshal. They're niggers," the leader said, evoking laughter from his followers. "Those niggers said they have a claim on a gold mine. We found them outside of Black Hawk. They were coming up here in their wagons just like white people. I never thought I'd see the day when niggers have prairie schooners and gold claims."

80

"That's not against the law, stranger. They're entitled to a claim and they can work…"

"Don't worry, marshal, they're going to work the claim. Only now it's our claim and they're going to do what niggers do best; be slaves for white men. And don't give me any of that talk about the law. There's no law here as far as I'm concerned. Now get out of my way before I walk right over you."

The marshal reached for his revolver. All twelve rifles were cocked and aimed at him. He halted his draw but repeated his request.

"You have the advantage now. You can go for your supplies and go to the livery. When you're finished I want you out of this town. But leave the Blacks here."

"You want the niggers? Take them. Take those nigger bitches and those piccaninnies. They've been following us all day. We're trying to get rid of them. Some of the boys wanted to shoot them like jackrabbits. But I wouldn't let them. The shooting might attract Indians. Take them with my blessings. But I'm not giving up those bucks. I need them for work."

I turned to ask Mister Hickok what he wanted to do. He was gone. I was scared but I was angry. I couldn't believe what was happening here. Slavery was abolished years ago. I remember as a little boy my mother reading a story in the newspaper about President Lincoln freeing the slaves.

These unfortunate Negro pioneers were the first Negro families in the Black Hills gold rush as far as I knew. But Negroes were all over the West. Many were in the Army, many were cowboys, and many were veterans of the Civil War. This had been a surprise to me when I came west. Despite all I read, I never read anything about Negro cowboys and soldiers.

I queried several newspapers back East to see if they'd be interested in a story on Negro cowboys. Only one editor wired back and he told me to forget it, pointing out that Negroes did not purchase or advertise in that paper. He did send me the address of a Negro newspaper in Philadelphia. I queried it but was informed it only accepted stories from Negro correspondents.

"Take these niggers and get them out of my way," the leader said and kicked at a little boy and girl who were standing near his horse.

"I took another quick look for Mister Hickok and began running towards the children, who thus far managed to evade the leader's boot by some artful dodging. Harry Young and Mister Langrishe grabbed me.

"Don't do anything foolish," said Harry Young. "They're holding all the cards now but I guarantee you not for long. Besides, nothing's going to happen to those kids. Look at them."

Quite true. The children were dodging and taunting the leader at the same time. Just then Kit ran into the street and pushed and shooed the children out of the way. Kittie and some of the whores took the children and Negro women by the arms and shoved them into the nearest open doors.

"You filthy son-of-a-bitch. If I had a gun I'd shoot you between your beady eyes," Kit yelled at the leader.

"When I settle in, I'll come back and visit you. I like them young and juicy," the leader said with a lustful leer that would even put General Custer to shame.

"You come anywhere near her and I'll cut off your cock and shove it down your throat," Kittie yelled.

Mother and daughter were dragged off the street by the marshal and several other men.

The leader chuckled and waved forward his small caravan. They traveled to near the top of the hill and turned off into a smaller side gulch. The big supply and outfitters store and the livery stable were located at the blind end of the small gulch. The Montana gang could usually be found at the livery stable.

Kit ran to me. Harry Young and Mister Langrishe were still holding me. They released me and I hugged Kit. She was in tears.

"I can't believe it. He ran out. He ran out like a ..."

Mister Hickok stepped out of the No. 10. He was dressed in his finest black suit, brocade vest, white silk shirt, string tie and black sombrero. He looked like a preacher. A very deadly preacher with his two Colts in their holsters, a thirty-two revolver in his waist band and the saloon's sawed-off, double-barrel, ten gauge shotgun in his right hand.

"I'm sorry, Bill. I couldn't..." the marshal began.

"Nothing to be sorry about. You did the right thing. A lot of innocent people would have died if you tried gunplay. That's why I waited. This is not the place to confront them."

Turning to Kit. "I'm proud of you. I know you hate scum like that as much as I do. My family didn't risk their lives protecting runaway slaves and being part of the Underground Railroad to allow a despicable deed such as this to take place so many years later."

He took the badge from the marshal's shirt. "Might as well make it official. All right, judge?"

The older, well-dressed man standing nearby nodded.

"Bill, do you want to swear in a posse and go in there?" the marshal asked.

"No. This can better be handled by myself. I don't want to create a crossfire situation. I still have bad moments when I think of poor Jim Williams in Abilene. I haven't killed a man since that tragic incident."

The shooting of Jim Williams was a great sorrow in Mister Hickok's life. The incident happened in September of Seventy-One and he still gets a little choked up speaking about it.

As I learned from several sources in Deadwood, the trouble began when Marshal Hickok closed down a crooked faro bank of Phil Coe, a gambler and particularly desperate person. Coe let it be known around Abilene he was out to get Marshal Hickok. And it was during the Dickinson County Fair, when most of the Texas cowboys were soaked with Valley Tan or Old Jordan whiskey, he made his move.

From what Harry Young told me, Marshal Hickok and his deputy, Jim Williams, were on the lookout for trouble at the Novelty Saloon when a shot was heard from the Alamo, a saloon across the street. Marshal Hickok ordered Williams to stay right where he was; he would look into it by himself.

He found Coe standing in front of the Alamo, revolver in hand. He asked Coe if he had fired the shot. Coe said yes and shot again at Marshal Hickok. The bullet grazed his side. He drew his revolvers, firing both simultaneously. Coe was struck in the abdomen, unusual since Marshal Hickok had a reputation as a head shooter.

Marshall Hickok turned quickly in anticipation Coe's friends would take up the fight. He saw a man running towards him with a pistol in each hand. Marshal Hickok fired one shot, this time in the head, and the man dropped. He was horrified to see he had killed his friend Williams.

"...I haven't killed a man since that tragic incident."

"But Jim disobeyed your orders. You told him to stay..." the marshal began.

"Yes and that's why I'm ordering you to keep everyone, yourself, foremost, away. I don't want anyone around. There won't be time to identify friend or foe if trouble begins."

I suspected that besides the memory of Jim Williams, Mister Hickok might have been worrying about his eyesight.

"Besides, there might not be any trouble. It would be better for one person to confront them and not force their backs to the wall. They may just listen to reason. I'll politely ask them to release the Negroes and leave town. In the meantime, everyone stay here. I am holding you responsible, marshal, to enforce this order."

"So, it will just be the three of us, huh?" asked Kit.

"No, young lady, you and Francis Scott will stay here and obey my orders like everyone else," Mister Hickok said as he mounted the marshal's horse and walked it slowly up Main Street.

"Get General Custer," the marshal said to me. "He's not bound to obey any orders."

"He should be in his dressing room," Mister Langrishe said, "entertaining his, what do you call them Kit? Groupers? Yes, groupers."

We were through the door of the theatre before the words left Mister Langrishe's mouth.

Kit threw a shoulder to the dressing room door, knocking the flimsy lock off its hasp.

"Don't you know enough to knock?" General Custer queried as he tried to pull a blanket over his naked body and the naked bodies of the two young women in bed with him.

Kit and the two young women giggled and smiled at each other.

Before the General had time to get further outraged, I explained the situation to him.

He sprang from the bed and began dressing rapidly. Not sloppily but with the quick precision of a soldier who has been doing this for years.

"Turn around, Kit, you're embarrassing your godfather."

The two young women were again uncovered but made no effort to hide their naked bodies, their curvaceous and firm naked bodies. They smiled at me. Kit spun me around.

"He's mine and don't forget it." Kit said with a smile. But a serious smile. Like the way Mister Hickok smiles when he's losing at cards.

"Let's go, Kit, we have to saddle the General's horse." I threw a wink at the two young women and got a punch in the arm for my effort.

General Custer kept his animals—horses, dogs, wild creatures, including a black bear—in a small barn behind the theatre. We quickly saddled and tacked out Bess, a recent addition to the menagerie, named in honor of the horse he lost at the Little Big Horn. I gently pushed Comanche aside to get at Ulysses.

General Custer ran to the barn and threw a repeating rifle at Kit. He leaped into the saddle just as Kit shoved the rifle in its sheath. He was in his stage clothing and looked, as usual, magnificent.

I grabbed Ulysses' mane and swung on his back. Kit took my extended arm and pulled up behind me.

"No, stay here. I know Bill doesn't want you around and neither do I." General Custer said as he spurred Bess towards the gulch.

"General Custer. You know I'm chronicling Mister Hickok and also keeping up to date notations in your journals. I'll write an accurate record of the event. You don't want Mister Stanley's account to be the only one?"

"Excellent point. But, Kit, you stay here."

"I have more right to be there than anyone and you know that, Uncle."

"I can't argue now. Keep behind me and stay out of the way."

We quickly reached the rim of the gulch. General Custer motioned us to stop and carefully peered over to keep out of sight. "Bill may have the situation under control. He's very deliberate when dealing with groups of troublemakers. If anyone can talk them out of gunplay, it's him."

And being deliberate was just what Mister Hickok was doing right now. He made a deliberate and elaborate motion of draping the reins of his horse over the scrub brush about a hundred feet from the front of the supply depot and the livery where the riders and Montana gang were standing, strung out along the front of the two buildings.

Mister Hickok made an elaborate production of breaking open the shotgun, removing its two cartridges, throwing them over his shoulder and inserting two fresh shells. He snapped the mechanism together quickly. The deadly metallic click could be heard distinctly on top of the gulch.

"Eighteen of them," General Custer said. "The Blacks aren't in sight. No doubt inside. That scum doesn't want them hurt. I may have to move fast. Keep back." He mounted Bess and crouched forward. Kit and I mounted Ulysses.

Mister Hickok could be seen walking slowly towards the two buildings. Again, his movements were deliberate. He stopped when he was about fifty feet from the leader.

"You had your little joke, boys, and everyone was amused. Now whey don't you just release those Negro gentlemen before I get the notion that you are actually serious."

"Well, well, what do we have here? The famous Wild Bill Hickok. I should have killed you back in Illinois when you were still a boy sneaking niggers up North."

"Many men have spoke those sentiments. But as you can see, I'm still here. But we shouldn't be standing under this hot sun talking of the good old days. Foremost on my mind right now is getting back to the saloon and having an iced-down beer while the ice is still holding out. Just release the Negroes and I'll be on my way and you could be on yours."

"If you want them that badly, walk through that door and get them," the leader said indicating a door in the middle of the line of men. Snorts and jeers.

"In time, in time. But now I just want to look at you. I didn't believe a man could get any uglier. Even under that dirt and crud, you're still ugly. Maybe I should have killed you when I was a boy. Where have you been hiding that ugly face all of these years? I would say down Mexico. A lot of people would like to see you. All of those fathers, brothers and sons of men you killed. You were the lowest and worst of the border guerrillas. Even Quantrill didn't want you around."

"That's a lot of big talk from a has-been gunslinger. But I appreciate the compliment. I was the worst. Didn't I tell you that boys? Only now I don't have to hide anymore. There's a hundred more men like this on their way to the Black Hills right now. Should be here in a day or two. Then I'm taking over these Indian lands before the government has a chance to act. I'm going to have my own state. Maybe my own country. I might be king…"

"You have been in the sun too long. King? That's the dumbest, goddamn thing I've heard in my life. Now, your highness, if you release the Negroes, you and your army can…"

"My offer still stands. If you want the niggers, get them."

"I'm sorry it comes down to this. There's no reasoning with you. You're not only crazy but also dangerous. Dangerous to the Black Hills and dangerous to my country." Mister Hickok began walking forward. "First I'm taking the Negroes, then…"

"You'll die trying, you bastard," he leader said as he turned his rifle on Mister Hickok.

Mister Hickok fired the shotgun as he continued walking. The leader was thrown back as the charge from one barrel hit him in the face, turning it into red meat and blood. He was dead before he hit the ground. Mister Hickok fired the other barrel at the rider standing nearest the door. The top of his head vanished.

Mister Hickok flung the shotgun at the men on the left and drew his Colts, firing on men both to his left and his right. Screams, gunfire, smoke and the pungent odor of black powder filled the air.

General Custer was now at full gallop approaching the supply depot.

"Yoooooooo," he shouted as he aimed his saber straightforward. Bess was shot from under him. As the horse rolled in death, General Custer leaped from the saddle and landed firmly on his feet in front of a group of men who now diverted their attention from Mister Hickok to him. The General slashed with his saber and fired with his side arm until the bloody bodies of six men lay in front of him.

Mister Hickok spun and shot the man who had just shot off his hat. There was no one left standing in front of the two buildings. There were some moans. Then there were some gunshots. All was quiet now.

Kit shouted to Ulysses to gallop forward and we were soon on the grisly scene. I felt a burning sensation in my throat but forced myself to swallow hard to avert an embarrassment.

As we jumped from Ulysses, Mister Hickok turned around and yelled for us to get away. Two men emerged from the doorway, Tim Brady and Johnny Varnes. I drew the Dragoon and aimed in their direction. I couldn't shoot. Mister Hickok was in the line of fire. I motioned him to get out of the way.

The two men fired as Mister Hickok jumped to the side. I felt my chest being slammed then a sharp pain in my stomach. As I fell backwards, the Dragoon flew in the air. Kit caught it by the handle with both hands. She fired twice immediately. One bullet went through the right eye of one of the men; the other put a hole in the forehead of the other.

I hit the ground. I tried to get up. I fell back again. Kit leaned over me. My eyes closed and the red whirlpool spun me around and around until...

...The fog moved in covering everything with a hazy whiteness; then it vanished leaving a dark void. The cycle kept repeating itself. Muted voices could be heard but not the words.

A cool, soothing, hand on my forehead. Kit, dearest Kit. Mother, sweet mother. Pain inside. Burning, searing pain. Falling, falling. Darkness. Black darkness. Faint light. Unbearable pain. The fog. The cool, soothing hand.

"Kit, darling, don't leave me. Take my hand. Don't let me fall. Hold me tighter."

The cool, soothing hand gripped my hand tighter. There was light behind the fog. The fog slowly drifted away. Burning, burning, bright light.

"Draw the curtains; the sunlight's hurting his eyes," a gruff voice commanded.

The cool, soothing, hand left.

"Please, please, come back."

The bright light vanished. The cool hand returned to mine.

"Thank you. Thank you." I kissed the hand. The hand was a blur but slowly came into focus. There was a shape beyond the hand. It grew clearer and clearer and...

"Welcome back, Francis Scott," said Martha Jane Cannary as she kissed my forehead. There were dark circles under her eyes and she began to cry softly.

"Don't start that slobbering now, Calamity. I told you I'd save him," said the gruff voice of Doctor Wesley, a real medical doctor and poker crony of Mister Hickok.

"Now, woman, can I have that drink?" Without waiting for an answer, Doctor Wesley poured a tumbler full with whiskey from a bottle on the table and drank it in one swallow. A sigh, another pour, another swallow, another sigh.

"Not a drink in three days. Three long days. Calamity said she'd shoot me if I had a drink while doctoring you. She'd wake me up every time you moaned and groaned. She saved you. Bill Hickok too for being smart enough to make her responsible for your life. Quite a woman. You know how she got that sobriquet? That came from nursing all those smallpox-inflicted pilgrims from a wagon train. No one else would go near it. She has a kind and generous heart. When people are sick, it's Calamity that takes care of them. Goddamn't, Calamity, if you'd take a bath and dress in some women's clothes, I'd take a poke at you myself." Another tumbler of whiskey downed.

"Don't pay attention to that bunk, Francis Scott. He saved your life. He cut your belly open and sewed away for hours. Everybody gave you up for dead. But Doc…"

"Be quiet, woman. He's just fortunate I had to operate on so many gunshot and arrow wounds in the Army. But I have to say, son, you were a challenge. The bullet in your abdomen tore up everything in sight—the alimentary canal, stomach, liver, spleen, kidney. I had a hell of a time sewing up all that stuff. Calamity was there all of the time. She did a lot of the fine sewing. Her eyes are better than mine and her hand steadier.

"The bullet in your chest is something else. It went in right between these two big ribs here. As luck would have it, it missed the arteries and the heart. It ended up against the lung on this side but didn't enter it. I can't do anything with it. Cutting in there would cause more damage and probably kill you. You'll have to carry that slug the rest of your life or until medical technology improves."

"What about Kit, Mister Hickok, General…"

"You'll learn soon enough, son. Give him some broth made from those herbs and roots you got from the Indians and have him rest," Doctor Wesley said as he walked to the door. "I'm repairing to the Number Ten. Don't send for me unless he's ready to kick the bucket."

"But Kit…"

"Hush, hush, Francis Scott, you'll learn all in due time. Now swallow some this broth."

The broth tasted wonderful as Martha Jane kept bringing big spoonfuls to my lips. It was soothing. So soothing…

"That's good, Francis Scott. Just close your eyes and sleep. You need rest, lots of…"

When I awoke, I couldn't wait to tell Kit what a wild and woolly dream I had. I tried to rise. I felt pain all though my chest and abdomen. Then I felt the thick roll of bandages covering most of my torso and realized it wasn't a dream. I felt weak, very weak. But my eyes were now focusing and I was alert to the noises around me. The sounds and voices of Deadwood Gulch outside the window, the ticking of the clock on the wall, the soft snoring of Martha Jane sleeping in a chair next to the bed.

Apparently Doctor Wesley's advice had been heeded. She was squeaky clean and wore a soft, cotton flowery dress. In her sleep, she looked much younger, probably only a couple of years older than myself.

She was holding my hand. I squeezed hers gently. She opened her eyes and smiled.

"Good morning, Francis Scott. You had a nice long sleep, almost twenty-four hours. You look like hell. How do you feel?"

"O.K., I guess. I'm alive. I should be thankful for that."

"Amen." She leaned over and kissed me on the lips. The way my mother kissed me. "I'll bet you're hungry? Hungry enough to eat a dead rat's ass," she said and ran out the door.

Well, maybe not quite that hungry. In fact, the thought of food did not appeal to me. I closed my eyes and thought of Kit.

"Don't you fall asleep. A don't want this food to get cold. Cooky was ready to send this meal to the dining room but I intercepted it."

She set a large tray on the table placed next to the bed and put a knife and fork in my hands.

"I don't want you to think I'm not appreciative, Martha Jane, but I don't feel like eating. I'm really not hungry. Maybe I should rest some more. Is that bacon? Well, maybe just a rasher or two. Ahh, nice and greasy, just the way I like it. That sausage smells good too. Put a couple of links on the plate with two or three biscuits. Better slide on some of those fried potatoes. No use letting those eggs get cold. Hard yokes. Great."

"Slow down. No one's going to take this food away from you. You want a bellyache. Har, har, that's a laugh isn't it?"

"How about a slice of that ham. The one with the big piece of fat on it."

"Doc said you could eat solid food, but I don't think he meant this much," she said as she plopped the slice of ham on the now empty plate.

"Uum, uum," was all I could manage in way of conversation. I couldn't stop eating. My stomach began hurting but I didn't stop until everything was gone. I was tempted to lick the grease off the platter but restrained myself.

A soft knock on the door. "It's me, Miss Jane."

"Come in, come in, he's awake now." And to me, "One of your guardians."

A Negro entered the room. He was one of the men who had been tied to the wagon. He looked different now. For one thing he had two revolvers around his waist.

"This is Mister Madison. His grandfather was a butler in the White House for President Madison. Isn't that true?"

"That's what he kept telling us," Mister Madison said and laughed. "But the truth is President Madison owned my grandfather. How's our boy doing? He looks about ready to jump on that big Percheron and ride East."

"He may just have to do that but we'll cross that bridge when we come to it."

"Thank you for helping us, young man," Mister Madison said as he gently shook my hand. "I don't know..." His voice trailed off.

"Don't worry about it. It was nothing. I don't mean it was nothing. I mean...I don't know what I mean. I'm confused..."

"No one can blame you for being confused. The shootout was four days ago and you just woke up. Mister Madison and the Negro men are taking turns watching the hotel, along with some of your other friends in town. They're guarding you in case..."

"In case?""

"I better start at the beginning and explain it all to you."

The beginning began after I had been shot.

"After Bill and George carried you to this room..."

And explain she did. The incident, like most things that happened in the West, got wilder and woollier with each telling. Most of this credit, or blame, could be given to the newspapers and in particular Mister Stanley, who, among other things, christened it "The Deadwood Massacre."

Twenty men in all had been killed. The marshal quickly determined that all of the deceased were wanted somewhere for various crimes, including murder. Facts soon fell by the wayside and the deceased were identified in many Eastern newspapers as pioneers instead of the dangerous scum they were. This is what usually happens when correspondents and reporters get their information third, fourth and even fifth hand. The number of dead also increased considerably. The figure quickly went from twenty to forty to eighty to one hundred.

Confusion, always newspapers' strongest ally, reigned supreme. After the shoot-out, Mister Hickok and General Custer gathered a posse and rode to the Indian treaty border of the Black Hills to intercept the one hundred or so men in the outlaw army heading this way.

Not a shot had to be fired to turn back the unwanted settlers. Mister Hickok and General Custer, always the showmen, had brought the recently deceased along with them. They warned the followers they would end up the same way if they insisted on entering the Hills. They wisely turned back but not before the dead were loaded in their wagons. This was the General's idea. Not only was a fight avoided but also a burial.

But somewhere along the way, the number of men in the wagon train got included in the casualty list. And, once more, President Grant's bowels were in an uproar. More so when it was discovered that the leader of this bunch of scum was a brother of a senator, a senator who supported the administration. Also, these "pioneers" had the blessings of several of the thieves in the administration.

President Grant ordered the capture of Mister Hickok and General Custer—dead or alive. But since the Black Hills were still not recognized as part of the United States there was the usual bureaucratic lack of action. The Army, however, was camped outside the boundary. The Legends of the West decided to make themselves scarce until the truth was known, if that were possible.

Events were also moving fast on the tin claim, which everyone agreed was a genuine bonanza. Kittie sold the whorehouse and was given a share to manage and develop the mining operation. A wise choice since neither Mister Hickok nor General Custer showed the least bit aptitude for business.

Although not involved in the incident, Kittie too thought it was wise to leave town. She was on her way to Denver to buy supplies and hire a mining engineer to sink a shaft.

My already spinning head was spinning even more trying to take in all of this information. Before I could ask a question, Martha Jane handed me a thick envelope. It was from Mister Hickok. I opened it and found a large wad of greenbacks and a letter. It read:

> *"Dear Son,*
>
> *I am proud of you and thank you for saving my life with the risk of yours. I remained in town long enough to see Doc Wesley complete the operation. He is confident you will live. He is even optimistic you are young enough and strong enough to recover completely. But don't get too anxious. He said you would have a long convalescence, at least a year and maybe even two.*
>
> *I want you to go back East to your college. George and I think it would be an ideal location for you to recover in peace. Also, since we couldn't find it on a map of Eastern United States, we doubt if anyone else could find it. There is a stack of sworn statements saying you weren't involved in the shootout. But President Grant and his cronies are angry and might try to arrest anyone close to George and me. You could even teach at college while you're gathering your strength. This way I know where to find you when I have to. Please do this for me and our darling Kit.*
>
> *The greenbacks are the money I had you pay to me and some more. I would never place a price on dear Kit's affections, even for college tuition and additional charges. I thought it would be a good way for you to save money and keep out of trouble. Kit has all the money she will ever need. And with this mine coming in, plenty more.*
>
> *I know you are now worried about Kit. Since she was involved in the shoot-out, we felt she too would have*

to disappear. She is now en route to an eastern college. No, not yours. I'm sorry but this will have to be kept a secret, even from you. Please, Son, don't try to find her. When the time is right, she will find you.

I am sorry I could not stay and see you on your way. I have made arrangements for your journey.

Take care, Young Pard, your friend always,
Bill.

Martha Jane handed me another envelope. This one much smaller. It read:

My Dearest Darling Franny,

I don't want to leave you but I must. I love you very, very, much and will be very sad until we are together again. I can't write anymore because it makes me cry. I will kiss you and kiss you until they drag me away. Don't fool around with any of those co-educational students at school or I'll shoot you between the eyes.

I love you,
Kit.

"Bill said the greenbacks will be better back East. A poke of gold would be too suspicious. And if you lived he wanted you to have these. He bought them brand new; they're not from any of those dead yahoos. He was going to use them himself but decided to stick with his old Colts."

A pair of new Colt Peacemakers in a custom belt with two holsters butts forward. I was so thrilled with the gift I almost forgot my wounds. Almost. I was too weak to hold it and it fell to the bed.

"Now you heed Bill and don't try to find Kit. She can take care of herself. And she can take care of you too. Don't try to fool around like George does to his sweet wife. Kit'll shoot you

95

for sure. By God, she took care of those two bozos. She's a real firecracker, just like her father."

"Her father?"

"I swear, Francis Scott, you're the dumbest man around. You went to college but you're too dumb to know that Bill's her father."

"Whose father?"

"Kit Carson Hickok's."

I really wasn't that dumb. I sort of suspected this but I wasn't going to be the one to bring it up. Still, I was thrilled by this information. But I didn't have time to dwell on it. Shouting from the street caught my attention.

"Jimmy, go out there and find out what's the commotion about," said Martha Jane,

He nodded and left.

"If it's what I think it is, we have to get you out of here fast."

"The Army's outside of town," Mister Madison yelled as he burst into the room. "The stage driver said it's the Fifth Cavalry. The marshal rode out to meet them. That's all anyone knows now."

"Get back to the tin claim right now, Jimmy. Take the other men with you. Stay out of sight until someone you can trust shows up. Now get."

"But, Miss Jane, the boy…"

"Get, I'll take care of him. I don't want to be worrying about you," she said as she pushed him out the door.

"By God, if this isn't the grandest sight I've seen in a long time," Martha Jane said as she looked out the window. "You'll have to see this." She practically carried me to the window.

Riding up Main Street on a big bay was one of the most impressive figures I have ever seen. Tall in the saddle and with a noble bearing was another Legend of the West: the Chief of Scouts, Buffalo Bill Cody. Clad in immaculate fringed buckskins, a spotless Stetson and high, glossy leather boots, he looked just as I expected him to look.

"Christ, he's a beautiful man," Martha Jane said.

He halted the bay in front of the hotel. He reached into a pouch at his side and pulled out what looked like a dead rat. He held it at arm's length above his head.

"First scalp for the Seventh Cavalry," he declared in a majestic timbre.

The crowd lining Main Street erupted into applause, shouts, hoots, whistles and gunshots. The demonstration lasted about five minutes until Colonel Cody silenced it.

"Thank you, thank you, you brave men of Deadwood. And let us not forget the whores," Colonel Cody added with a majestic sweep of his hat to the women standing outside the nearby whorehouses. "But I am not here for applause for killing Yellow Hand." Another spontaneous demonstration that too had to be silenced by Colonel Cody. But not before it went on for another five minutes.

"And I am not here to make a speech…"

Perhaps a speech was not his intention but with a little encouragement from his audience, the great buffalo hunter, scout and showman launched into a narrative that began at Cheyenne, Wyoming, with General Wesley Merritt and the Fifth Cavalry, and concluded three weeks later at War Bonnet Creek. It was an interesting story that no doubt would play well in the East. Hell, it was even playing well in the West. Martha Jane reluctantly gave me a tablet and pencil. This too was part of the record.

The Army was in pursuit of a band of eight hundred southern Cheyenne who left the reservation at Red Cloud to join Sitting Bull. General Merritt, having been informed of the Cheyenne's intention and position by Colonel Cody and his scouts, decided he must prevent the Cheyenne forces from joining the Sioux. He did this at risk of a court martial for disobeying orders to join General Crook at Fort Laramie. But it was on this day they had learned of the massacre of the Seventh Cavalry at the Little Big Horn.

Colonel Cody, the next morning at daybreak, reported to General Merritt the Cheyenne were heading towards War Bonnet Creek. General Merritt ordered his command to mount and mass under the bluffs.

Colonel Cody had the honor of leading the signal party at a nearby hill. In addition to him, his party consisted of two scouts, Tait and Buffalo Chips White, and six troopers. Other troopers crouched out of sight on the slope ready to pass along the signal.

"The Cheyenne were resplendent in their war dress and approached us with the sun flashing on their polished armlets and lance heads. With gaily painted rawhide shields, and the wind streaming their long war bonnets behind them, I was the first to note an unusual activity among the Cheyenne. On their flank a group of seven warriors were so intent on collecting the scalps of two couriers they did not notice us as they galloped towards us. I recognized an opportunity!" Colonel Cody exclaimed to his awed audience. " 'By Jove! General, now's our chance! Let our war party mount here and we can cut those fellows off!' "

" 'Up with you then,' " ordered General Merritt.

"With a cheer I led my little band against the Indians' flank. They sprang from their horses and met our daring charge with a volley. Yellow Hand singled me out as a foe worthy of his steel. We saw each other simultaneously. It is certain we fired at the same instant. My shot pierced his leg. I was not hit but at the same moment my horse stepped into a gopher hole and threw me. I jumped to my feet, recovered my rifle, and fired again, killing Yellow Hand! We were not more than fifty feet apart. I rushed forward, and for the benefit of the oncoming troopers, raised the savage's war bonnet into the air and shouted, 'First scalp for the Seventh.' The soldiers responded with cheers as they galloped past."

As did his Deadwood audience. Another display of applause, shouts, hoots, whistles and gunshots. This time it took him longer to silence the demonstration. Perhaps he needed to catch his breath.

"Thank you, thank you. General Merritt is ready to ride into Deadwood as soon as I conclude important business. I want you to welcome him as you did me. He is a good man! It is he who sent me into this now famous town to warn anyone who was witness to the alleged deed or friends of Bill Hickok and George Custer to leave town immediately. There are federal marshals and other assorted Washington troublemakers riding with the Fifth Cavalry. But General Merritt will not allow them to proceed until I ride back and report to him. "But before anyone leaves," he added, halting many persons already in motion, "I have more to my story." More applause but this was quickly waved down.

"I hear there's some accounts going around that my duel with Yellow Hand ended with me yielding a Bowie knife and him coming at me with a tomahawk. Don't you believe it. What I told you was the truth; witnessed by dozens of officers and men of the Fifth. That other account is plain bunk and I will not be a participant in spreading untruths about myself!"

This time Colonel Cody waved his arm before the outbreak began.

"And another misconception I want to make straight. This is about the scalping." Again holding up what looked like a dead rat. Again applause. Again a wave of silence. "I have been reading accounts of those misguided women and soft-headed men back East that I was wrong in taking the scalp of Yellow Hand."

Boos and protests.

"Maybe the white man has treated his Indian brother badly in some respects. But from the accounts I heard from the Little Big Horn, the Indians are lucky any of them have scalps."

More cheers.

"I want everyone to know I never scalped an Indian before. But after I removed the war bonnet and looked down at Yellow Hand, I saw things that almost turned my stomach. There wrapped around his groin was an American flag used as a breech clothe. Imagine his filthy ballocks and cock rubbing against Old Glory. And if that wasn't bad enough, attached to the hair on his head was the scalp of a blonde woman."

Anger from the audience.

"These sights so infuriated me that I forthwith scalped the heathen dog! By this time the Fifth had engaged the Cheyenne and had them running helter-skelter to the reservation. The sight of me killing Yellow Hand was too much for them. This allowed me time to do the proper ceremonies. I burnt to ashes the desecrated flag and gave the blonde scalp a Christian burial!"

Applause and cheers, this time dying down rapidly as dozens of men, women and whores began leaving town.

"Now if someone will kindly direct me to the Deadwood Hotel," said the Chief of Scouts, who was standing in front of it. "I'm looking for..."

"Up here, Bill, you handsome devil," yelled Martha Jane. "And don't detour to some whorehouse. You want anything, I got it right up here. And free."

Cheers and laughter from the now diminished crowd.

Colonel Cody was in the room in no time. "We got to hurry, Jane, we got to hurry. General Merritt can't hold back those federal marshals forever. Bill Hickok asked me to...Christ, Jane, this is the best I've ever seen you look. And you smell good too."

Martha Jane turned into a coquette and Colonel Cody a randy boy as they hugged with the Colonel copping a couple of feels here and there.

"We can discuss this further, Jane, after I finish my duties here," he said as he shoved her away. I didn't think I'd ever escape from that crowd. But that's the price of fame," he sighed as he gingerly lowered himself into the big parlor chair.

"Christ, that's the best thing my ass felt in a long time. I'm telling you, Jane, it isn't easy to be a legend. I've been riding over the territories for a month now chasing those goddamn Indians. And for what? An opportunity to get killed? I can't believe it. I had to fight the only Cheyenne that was willing to fight. At the first sight of the Army, the other Cheyenne were falling over each other trying to get back to the reservation. But not Yellow Hand. That bastard had to stand and fight. I'm getting too old for Indian fighting. I'm thirty years old now. Thirty-fucking-years old. I'm practically an old man."

"You look wonderful, Bill. You're still the handsomest man around. Well, one of the handsomest. And you don't look a day over twenty-five."

"You think so," Colonel Cody said as he scrutinized his image in the hand mirror Martha Jane held up to him. "Well, my face doesn't look old but my body feels it. Too long in the saddle. Everything aches. Maybe I should spend more time on the stage and less time in the sage."

"You should. You were born for the stage. You can draw a crowd anywhere you go."

"Yes, the stage is certainly a more attractive alternative than Indian fighting. And it pays much better too. If only I didn't feel like such a goddamn fool. I'm so bad on stage it's an embarrassment to me. I remember back in Seventy-Two I was doing Ned Buntline's 'Scout of the Plains' in the Saint Louis Grand Opera House. Ned was there and Texas Jack. I could never remember my lines. Ned had to prompt me all the time. I looked out into the audience and saw Louisa with her family. 'Oh, Mama, I'm a bad actor!' I yelled to her."

Colonel Cody even had to stop his complaining to laugh.

"That Louisa. She'll send me to an early grave. That woman does nothing but nag. Nag, nag, nag, nag. And jealous. If a nubile girl is within eyesight, she immediately assumes I'm going to fuck her."

"Aren't you?"

"That's not the point, Jane. She's getting so bad that Indian fighting is preferable to being with her. And she's the one who insists I perform on the stage. If it were up to her, she'd have me give up everything and devote my life to show…ahh…show business. And she sews those foppish costumes for me and forces me to wear them."

"Your buckskins are as handsome as you. Surely…"

"She didn't make this outfit. Some young girl I know in…well…that doesn't really matter. Louisa's creations aren't this tasteful and restrained. You should see what she had me wear on this campaign. It was an outrageously ornate black velvet and gold Mex-cowboy uniform. It was ornamented with silver lace and buttons and slashed with crimson. I looked like a valquero pimp. I'm sure that goddamn costume was why Yellow Hand stayed around to fight. That bastard was even laughing at me and pointing me out to the other Cheyenne. Fortunately that costume got ruined at the battle. When I fell from my horse, the crotch seams split right open and…"

"I wish I was there to see that, Bill."

"In due time, Jane. The crotch opened up and there I was with my ballocks flapping in the breeze. I swear Yellow Hand was laughing so hard he missed his shot. Then I got it all bloody when I scalped that bastard. There are a couple of artists doing paintings on the duel. I told them all if they put me in that pimp suit I'd shoot them. I want to be portrayed in the usual habiliment of a scout, fringed buckskins."

"Is that really the scalp of Yellow Hand?" Martha Jane asked, pointing to the pouch at his waist.

"No. I sent the war bonnet, bridle, whip, arms and his scalp to Rochester so Louisa can show the neighbors. This is a rat I shot on the way to Deadwood."

For the first time, Colonel Cody acknowledged me.

"This the boy Bill wants back East?"

He looked me over and from his expression was under whelmed by what he saw. I couldn't blame him. I had been looking in the big mirror on the dresser and was not very impressed myself. I was ghostly white, had lost about twenty pounds and my hair was sticking up in clumps. I didn't look much better than the rat in the pouch.

"Don't just stand there with you thumb up your ass, we have to get moving," he said but made no effort to rise from the chair. "Christ," I'm tired. My health is not very good. Working myself to death. And what do I have to show for it? I shot scores of Indians and I have only one scalp to call my own. One lousy scalp."

"But it is a very important scalp, Sir. A scalp that will surely go down in Western lore. I even plan to include the duel in my journals of Mister Hickok."

"Journals of Mister Hickok?" he asked with interest.

"That's right, Bill, Francis Scott is keeping Bill's records. And he's a good writer too. Not like that goddamn Ned Buntline or that windbag Henry Stanley. He looks like death warmed over but he's a good young man. Bill treats him like a son. And him and Kit…"

"Kit?"

102

"Yes, Kit. Bill Hickok's daughter. You know her. Kit Carson Hickok. Your own...ohh...I'm sorry, Bill."

Colonel Cody fell back in the chair. He closed his eyes tightly but little streams of tears managed to run out the corners.

"Bill, poor Bill. You go ahead and cry. You deserve it," Martha Jane said as she sat on an arm of the chair and hugged him.

I knew part of the reason for Colonel Cody's breakdown was prompted by something they were just beginning to call fatigue. But I also knew it was because of a great personal loss. Mister Hickok and Kittie talked about it one night after Mister Hickok received a letter from Colonel Cody.

Colonel Cody had three children, his two daughters, Arta and Orra, and his son Kit Carson Cody. He, like Mister Hickok's daughter, was named for the famous frontier scout Kit Carson whom both men knew and admired.

From what I learned and recorded, Kit Carson Cody was a handsome boy with a somewhat poetic look. He had his father's eyes and hair and was extremely sensitive. Unlike his father, he loved the stage. When the curtain rose, and there was a full audience, he would yell to his father, "Good house, Papa!"

This past April, as he was ready to go on stage in Springfield, Massachusetts, Colonel Cody was handed a telegram. It was from Louisa. Kit was seriously ill with scarlet fever. He caught a train to Rochester but by the time he reached home, his beloved son was clinging to life.

He was told by doctors there was no hope. He took his son in his arms and held him throughout the night. There Kit Carson Cody died. He was not yet six years old. Mister Hickok said Colonel Cody loved all children but above all his only son.

"That's right. You just go to sleep now," Martha Jane said as she gently released Colonel Cody and folded his arms in front of him. "He's just tired, Francis Scott, bone tired. He's been set up on a pedestal and feels he has to live up to his reputation. But with all that bunk being written by Ned and those other dime novelists, it is even hard for him to know just what it is he's suppose to be living up to."

Martha Jane walked over to me and placed a hand on my forehead. "I've been neglecting you, my poor dear. You feel cool and you're getting some color back. I know you should be in bed for a couple of weeks but I ain't got a choice now. I have to get us on the road. I'm going over to see Jack Langrishe about our rig. Sit in this chair and get comfortable. Keep an eye on the Colonel. Here, reach over the side. That's your journals. I read them while I was sitting by your bed. God knows how. Your handwriting's like chicken scratch. I'm thinking about writing my own book and I got some notions how you should write yours," she said as she left the room.

Everybody's a critic, I thought as I lifted the leather pouch containing the dozen or so tablets. Martha Jane's right. I could just about decipher my handwriting. I had been told it was something to do with being left-handed. Even so, I was now more impressed by the words spoken by Mister Hickok. There were several passages about Kit, nothing about what we really did, but rather how her life was woven into the fabric of Mister Hickok's.

Father and daughter. I think I even loved them more for that. Christ, how I missed them. I felt a part of me had been taken away. But maybe it was just all that stuff Doctor Wesley removed.

Colonel Cody began to stir. I scrutinized him closely for the first time. I had to agree with Martha Jane. He was a beautiful man.

He awoke, leaped out of bed—one hand on a pistol butt, the other on a knife—and looked ready to fight.

"Where's Jane?"

"She went to get a rig from Mister Langrishe. He has the theatre next to the Number Ten. That's where General Custer performed his narrative."

He became interested in General Custer's act and more so when I explained it to him in detail.

"Sounds grand. I'm only sorry I can't hang around to do some narrative performances myself. I could do the Battle of War Bonnet Creek. Not for myself, of course, but as a duty to future generations. It might do me good to perform before frontier patrons. I've been performing for dudes so long I may be losing the real spirit of the West. And I'm sure those pulchritudinous young women…"

He paused. A lustful leer appeared.

"So, George Custer has a successful act? I shouldn't doubt it. He has always been a dramatic personage in word and deed. What a draw the three of us would be—Cody, Custer and Hickok. Maybe by now, Bill, whom I love like a brother, would be more receptive to the footlights. He toured with my stage company for a brief interlude. He was a disaster. Did he tell you much about it? I'd like to see what he has to say."

"No, Sir. He mentioned it briefly but never elaborated."

This wasn't quite true but I didn't want to get Colonel Cody riled. In fact, I had a tablet open to that particular episode of Mister Hickok's life.

As much as I loved Mister Hickok, I had to admit he was a real pain-in-the-ass to Colonel Cody. The first time he performed he spat out the tea that was in the whiskey bottle the boys were passing around the campfire while telling lies to the audience and demanded real whiskey.

In his own words:

"You must think I'm the worst fool east of the Rockies, that I can't tell whiskey from cold tea. This don't count and I can't tell a story under the temptation unless I get real whiskey."

To pacify him, Colonel Cody sent out for a bottle. The audience howled. But at least the whiskey loosened up Mister Hickok's tongue. It also made him amorous with the leading lady.

"I didn't think I could get through this one scene if I didn't have half a snootful. Imagine this. A band of Indian warriors had stolen a pale-face maiden and ran off with her. I dashed to the rescue, blazing away and at every bark of my pistol, a redskin drops. Finally when there are dead redskins all about the stage, I strike an heroic attitude and clasp the maiden to my breast and say: 'Fear not, fair maid, by heavens, you are safe at last with Wild Bill, who is ready to risk his life and die if need be in the defense of weak and helpless womanhood.' "

105

There was probably some justification for Mister Hickok's behavior on stage but it was difficult to rationalize his treatment of the supernumeraries. In the sham Indian battles, he was supposed to shoot over the heads of the supers so not to cause injury. Real ammunition, of course, was not used but the powder and wad of the blank cartridge could cause a good sting if fired too closely.

In his words:

"Well, what I did after awhile was to put my revolver close to the supers' legs and fire and burn them. This would make them dance and jump so that it was difficult to make them fall and die. I sometimes did this to prolong the play. They were being paid twenty-five cents a performance for this dying business but none of them wanted to die. I guess I can't blame them. Those powder charges must have stung unmercifully."

This was not Mister Hickok's most sensitive period.

"No, Sir. He mentioned it briefly but never elaborated."

"I'm not surprised. Bill Hickok's no showman and he's even a sorrier businessman. But he must have mentioned something about his Wild West Show?"

"Not a lot. He mentioned he took real buffalo and Indians to Buffalo and Niagara Falls."

"I'm surprised."

I was surprised myself when Mister Hickok related the incident. But he was half in the bag. Later he told me never to tell anyone about the Wild West Show or...The "or" was enough for me. The idea was excellent but he just had bad luck.

Mister Hickok knew the Wild West was of big interest in the Easy East. He had no difficulty rounding up cooperative Indians but capturing wild buffalo was another story. He was used to shooting them, not making pets of them. The show was open in the spring of Seventy.

In his words:

"The venture not only failed miserably, it failed spectacularly. I just never resolved the logistics of presenting the show outdoors and charging admission. Getting the buffalo into the arena almost caused a riot. The beasts got away from the Indians and were running everywhere but where I wanted them

106

to run. The Indians were chasing them and yapping dogs and yelling children chasing the Indians. If all of this wasn't bad enough, a grizzly bear from the sideshow got out of its cage in the railroad car. He smelled some sausage a vendor was hawking and went after it. The vendor took off faster than the buffalo and the grizzly ate all his fare. We finally herded the buffalo into a dead-end street and got them under control. By now it was too late. The people coming to the show saw the accidental buffalo hunt for nothing and weren't about to pay anything. There was a lot of damage and I had to sell the buffalo to pay it off and raise train fare to get myself and my Indians back to the Plains. I figured there had to be a better business than show business."

"I'm surprised," Colonel Cody repeated, "he didn't say much about it. I thought it was the best idea he ever had. A genuine Wild West Show. I've been giving the idea a lot of attention. I could get real Indians and buffalo. And cowboys, sharpshooters, soldiers, trick riders. A panorama of the true West before it becomes an extension of the East. You know how those New York people ruin everything! I'll put under contract some famous Indians before we kill them off. Like that Sitting Bull fellow and Crazy Horse. They'd draw in those dudes in droves."

"But they just massacred the Seventh Cavalry."

"Now you're catching on. I could stage a battle of Last Stand Hill and come to the rescue. I would be the greatest show on earth."

He pointed his arm out, peered into the distance, and struck a theatrical pose. He turned and winked. "All bunk, isn't it? I swear I better stop reading those stories about myself. Maybe when you're back East you can start on my journals. I was thinking of writing my autobiography but I haven't time now. I honestly want the world to know the truth about me."

"I'd be honored, Sir. Mister Hickok has already told me much about you. I assure you, you have a prominent place in his journals."

"What did he say? I want to read it. Is that part of the journal?"

I handed him the tablet knowing he would not be able to read my handwriting.

107

"I can't read this."

"Neither can I," I said, peering at the tablet he handed back to me. "But I assure you, everything Mister Hickok said about you is complimentary." I may have been weak, I may have been confused. But I wasn't weak or confused enough to allow Colonel Cody to see what was in Mister Hickok's journals. I did not need another editor.

"Young man, I assure you I am not completely insensitive. I realize even scriveners have some sense of pride. I will not interfere in Bill's literary efforts. But I just want to make sure all the facts concerning me are correct. But enough of this. Get dressed. We're going to the Number Ten to see Jane. And maybe I could have a talk with this Jack Langrishe."

I started to protest, telling him I didn't think I could stand. But he wouldn't hear it. In pain that almost doubled me over I walked to the dresser and poured water from the pitcher into a basin. I was clean, Martha Jane saw to that, but I wanted to splash some water on my face. I also soaked my hair so I could comb it. I began to feel a little better.

"I was shot a couple of times. Doc Wesley has me all sewn up. He says I'm lucky to be alive. I…"

"Ahh, that's nothing. When I was with the Pony Express…"

God save me from another Pony Express story. But my God was apparently not listening. Colonel Cody went on about how he had to continue to ride despite looking like a pincushion with all the arrows sticking out of him. And all the time hundreds of Indians were in pursuit.

The Pony Express was only in business from 1860 to 1861. But it seemed everyone I met had something to do with it. Men who were now thirty were riders, while youth under twenty were stable boys. Even the fifteen-year-old towel boy at Kittie's told me he watered the horses.

During its brief tenure, the Pony Express performed a dangerous and valuable service. It delivered mail from Saint Joe, Missouri, to Sacramento, California. A total of 1,960 miles in only ten days. But with all of the men and boys claiming to be involved, there should have been no need for ponies. They could have stood side-by-side for the entire 1,960 miles, passing the letters hand-to-hand.

"...No little scratches like yours. Us lads of the Pony Express were tough. Not like today's milksops. I remember little Will Simpson riding his stretch with an Indian spear completely through him..."

I listened to Colonel Cody's bunk while I dressed. I could use a hand but he was using both of his patting himself on the back. At least I had some fancy clothes to wear since Mister Hickok had to leave most of his. I chose his black suit, gold brocade vest, white ruffle-front shirt and string tie. The pants wouldn't stay up because I lost so much weight. Strapping on the Peacemakers solved this. Now the problem was I couldn't walk because the guns were so heavy.

"...And Alf Slade—he was known as Terrible Slade for his habit of shooting men who didn't agree with him—fought off a dozen Indians with a tomahawk sticking out of his head..."

I looked in the mirror and got frightened by what stared back. Death staring at death.

"...I met Bill Hickok on the Pony Express. He was about ten years older than me. A tall, handsome blond with long hair, a long curly moustache and sharp blue eyes. He looked like a god to me. Even then he was a virtuoso with a Colt." He looked at me and paused. "By god, Son, you gave me a fright. Is that Bill's suit and guns?"

"The clothes are his but the guns are mine. He gave them to me." I drew the revolvers, twirled them until they faced butt forward, and offered them to Colonel Cody for his examination.

"Peacemakers. I haven't seen many, especially a matched pair. Want to sell them?"

I quickly retrieved the weapons before he got attached to them.

"Yes, I understand. They are a gift from Bill. But if you ever want..."

I took several steps and almost lost my balance. My legs were independent of my will. I reached out for Colonel Cody. He stepped back.

"I don't want to pamper you, Son," he said as he opened the door and motioned me to walk out.

I fell to the floor and not so softly cursed Colonel Cody for his misguided attempt to build my character.

"I can't make it to the Number Ten. Hell, I can't even make it to the door. You go by yourself. But don't forget to tell Martha Jane you left me floundering on the floor. I will when I see her."

"Well, maybe I should give you a hand. Bill Hickok did say you were badly shot up." He effortlessly picked me up and practically carried me on his hip down the flight of steps to the front door.

The bright sunlight caused me to blink as I navigated across the street. Colonel Cody had left me so he could press the flesh with his admirers. I thought I'd double over from the pain inside but at least now my legs were working.

"...I stared at that enemy of mine—that enemy of all Americans. Bitter fluids gorged my throat when I saw the Stars and Stripes wrapped around his filthy crotch and the long yellow hair of a white woman..."

Two miners must have sensed by unsteadiness as they grabbed me under my arms and lifted me to the door of the No. 10.

"That won't be necessary, gentlemen," Colonel Cody said as he relieved them of their burden and took me through the door. He immediately released me after making sure everybody witnessed his deed of mercy.

"What the hell are you doing here?" Doctor Wesley yelled from the card table. "You shouldn't be up and around yet. I didn't spend all that time repairing your entrails so you could kill yourself for being so goddamn stupid." He stood and started to walk towards me. Captain Massey tugged on his sleeve and told him it was his bid. Doctor Wesley sat down again and examined his cards.

"What the hell are you doing here?" Martha Jane yelled as she and Mister Langrishe rushed towards me and sat me down. "And shame on you, Bill Cody. You should have taken care of him."

"I couldn't help it, honest, Jane. He insisted we come here. I couldn't stop him. Right, Son?"

"Bunk," Martha Jane said and fussed over me.

"Ahh, Mister Langrishe, I assume," Colonel Cody said as he took the hand of that gentleman. "Could we have a little talk? It could prove to be profitable for both of us. I understand George Custer packed the house with his..." The voice trailed off as they walked through the theatre's entrance.

"Calamity said you're leaving us," Harry Young said as he set down two schooners of beer and a salt shaker. "I'll miss our conversations. No one left to talk to but these bozos," he added, waving an arm around the saloon. "You look good for a man who came so close to death. Nice suit."

"Thank you. It's Mister Hickok's."

"Thought I recognized it."

"Don't give that boy anything to drink, goddamn't," Doctor Wesley yelled over.

"Only beer, Doc. He needs some beer and salt to get over his dehydration," Harry Young said.

"Everyone's a goddamn physician in this place," Doctor Wesley said. "Just two or three. Don't overdo it," he added and went back to his card playing.

"I don't know, Mister Young. I really don't think I want beer now. Maybe a glass of milk or..."

"Just drink. It'll be good for you," he said as he helped me lift the schooner to my lips.

The beer tasted great. I was half in the bag before the schooner returned to the table.

"There's a letter here that has to be answered," Harry Young said, suddenly becoming very solemn. "I'd like to do it myself but you know I'm writing my own book and haven't time. And since you're a newspaper correspondent I thought you might..."

"Certainly, Mister Young."

He handed me an envelope and hurried back to the bar. The letter was addressed to No. 10 Saloon, Deadwood, Dakota Territory. It was posted from Louisville, Kentucky.

The letter read:

To Whom It May Concern:
Dear Sir,

I saw in the newspaper a piece about the death of Jack McCall in your business establishment. There was a young man of the name of John McCall left here about six years ago, who has not been heard of for the last three years. He has a father, mother and three sisters living here in Louisville, who are very uneasy about him since they heard of the shooting of Jack McCall. If you can send us any information about him, we would be thankful to you.

This John McCall is about twenty-five years old, has light hair, inclined to curl, and one eye crossed. I cannot say about his height, as he was not grown when he left here. Please write as soon as convenient, as we are very anxious to hear from you.

Very respectfully yours,
Mary A. McCall
(Sister of John McCall)

"Are you all right, dear?" Martha Jane asked as she placed her hand on my forehead. "You looked pained."

I handed her the letter. She read it slowly and aloud. With all of the usual saloon noise, it was doubtful if anyone else could hear her.

"You sometimes forget even a miserable, ugly, sneaky creature like Broken Nose has folks someplace who love him. I truly feel sorrow for them. Especially this poor girl who wrote this letter."

As in indication of her sorrow, several tears dropped from her eyes and a small glob of snot gathered at the bottom of her nose. She was about to wipe it off on the sleeve of her clean dress, apparently thought better of it, yanked at the kerchief around the neck of the cowboy sitting at the next table, almost yanking him off his stool, and wiped her nose on that.

"But in God's truth, Francis Scott, I'd rather be reading this kind of letter from Jack McCall's sister then from Bill Hickok's sister."

"Amen," said Harry Young as he set before us two more schooners of beer. From his tray, he removed a sheet of paper, an envelope, pen, bottle of ink, and arranged them neatly before me after wiping the table clean with his apron.

"Harry, how about cleaning up this table, it looks like a bear shit on it. And bring us a fresh bottle of that varnish you're passing off as whiskey," requested a neighbor.

"Clean it up yourself, you slobber. And this isn't Delmonico's. If you want something, go to the bar and get it," Harry Young said with a hint of indignation as he walked back to the bar.

I picked up the pen, dipped its nib in the bottle of ink, shook it off on the sawdust-covered floor and dipped it in again. I quickly wrote the letter and addressed the envelope. I waved both of them in the air to dry the ink, folded the paper and placed it in the envelope. Harry Young was back.

"I'll seal it and apply the postage," he said.

"Hold on, I didn't have a chance to read it," Martha Jane said as she reached for the envelope.

I gently took her hand. "No use both of us reading it." I really didn't want anyone to read what I wrote. "I had to tell the truth. If her brother didn't die, another man would have. Not a lot of good tidings for his people in Louisville. I promised, though, he would have a headstone and it would read he was loved by his family. I'll give you some money, Mister Young, to…"

"You did your part, Mister Roche," he said waving away my offer. "I'll pass the hat. Maybe his family will come here some day to see his grave."

Before it became necessary to comment further on the subject, the unmistakable voice of Colonel Cody penetrated the noise, silencing it instantly. He stood on a stool in the doorway to the theatre and once again told of his duel with Yellow Hand.

I didn't pay too much attention since I heard it so many times I could recite it myself. Besides, I was thinking of Kit. My dear, sweet, delicious Kit. My paramour. My lover. My…my God. What the hell is that ham saying?

"…Our eyes locked in combat across the purple plain. We dismounted at the same time, never taking our eyes off each other. Neither of us blinking. Finally he whooped and cried out, "Oh great buffalo hunter whose long shadow casts over the Indian nation, I fear you not even though you are a living legend and of greater fame than even the one we call Son of the Morning Star.'

"I looked skyward and yelled: 'This is for you; you brave men of the Seventh Cavalry. You who died in glory. You gracious dead.' We charged each other. Yellow Hand's tomahawk raised high and glistening in the sun; my Bowie knife turned upward…"

Martha Jane and I looked at each other. We were accustom to bunk but this was above and beyond the call of duty.

"…Our bodies clashed. His tomahawk grazed my head but I shook off the pain and planted the Bowie to the hilt in his red belly. He looked at me with disbelief in his eyes. I smiled and twisted the blade. 'Die slowly, you Cheyenne cur…' "

I caught Colonel Cody's eye. He shrugged his eyebrows and broke into a possum-eating-shit grin.

"So much for the world knowing the truth about Colonel Cody," I said to Martha Jane as we joined the applause.

"Don't be hard on him. He's smart enough to now that people don't want to know the truth. Or at least all of it. Bunk is more interesting. And much more fun."

"…Covering his filthy ballocks was Old Glory. I thought of those inspirational words of that great American writer, Francis Scott…"

I started to rise. Martha Jane was right. Bunk is much more fun.

"…Key"

I slinked back into my seat.

"…Whose bright stars and red stripes…"

All stood as he sang in his rich baritone voice and waved the American flag. It was a very dramatic moment. The electricity of lightning seemed to fill the air. Even I, who knew it was all

114

bunk, had a lump in my throat and a tear in my eye. What showmanship. Even General Custer, who left no stone of maudlin patriotism unturned, hadn't thought of singing Mister Key's poem and waving the flag.

Standing in the doorway of the saloon with a look of urgency and incongruity was the marshal. It was obvious he wanted to rush to Colonel Cody but couldn't while he was still singing and waving the flag.

At last.

"…And the home of the brave."

While the house rocked with applause, hoots and stomping, the marshal ran over and grabbed Colonel Cody.

"Bill, you have to get moving. General Merritt dispatched me to tell you he can't wait any longer—he got a bunch of newspaper correspondents with him and they're all complaining about their deadlines. He said he's moving out the Fifth," quickly consulting a big hunter case watch, "about now."

Sure enough, the faint strains of Garryowen could be heard.

"Their graves aren't even cold yet and the Fifth has stolen the Seventh's march," Colonel Cody said.

"No, the Fifth is playing it in tribute. But let's not get sidetracked. You have to get Calamity and Francis Scott out of Deadwood. The federal marshal has warrants on them."

Colonel Cody was oblivious to the marshal's plea as he affixed his signature to a stack of portrait photographs that suddenly appeared on the table in front of him. His fanatics were eagerly paying a silver dollar for the privilege of owning this memento.

"Let's go, Bill. Now."

"General Merritt knows full well I am not only carrying out his orders but he wishes of my good friends and those great Americans, General George Armstrong Custer and Wild Bill Hickok, who have entrusted me with the well being of these two…"

"And he said not to allow you to make any more speeches," the marshal said and again urged Colonel Cody to get going. The marshal and Mister Langrishe stood me up. Each grabbed an arm and walked me across the floor. Martha Jane pushed patrons aside as we made our egress. Colonel Cody was now on his feet and began walking swiftly; perhaps because of the urgency of the situation—Garryowen was growing louder. But more than likely because he exhausted his supply of photographs.

Waiting outside was Mister Langrishe's personal tour wagon, which he used when he took his act throughout the territory. It had a top and rolled-down canvas sides. The inside was lined with a mattress. The rig was extremely comfortable. Kit and I could attest to that. After a performance, Mister Langrishe would sleep in the back while Ulysses took him to the next stop.

"Ulysses," I shouted. He turned, looked at me, and winked. I swear.

Tied to the back of the rig were Tall Bull, Colonel Cody's bay, and Choctaw, Martha Jane's Indian pony. Our baggage was already piled inside. Whores from Kittie's former establishment were lining the coach with pillows and baskets of food.

"I am relegating the responsibility of Ulysses' welfare to you, Mister Roche," Mister Langrishe said as he and the marshal eased me through the back flap of the coach. "I would like to have him back but if that proves impossible, you keep him," he waved aside my thanks. "Mister Hickok remunerated me for him and the coach. But I only agreed to part with him under the agreement you would keep him and take good care of him."

I assured him I would.

"Calamity said the three of you will be heading for Colonel Cody's spread at North Platte, Nebraska. From there riverboat and rail back East. Don't let him connive that noble beast away from you. And make sure Calamity doesn't sell him.

"For chrissake, Jack, he's only a goddamn horse," Martha Jane said.

Snorts from Ulysses.

"Don't worry, I'll take care of that precious horse, Jack," Martha Jane said and whispered in my ear, as she tucked one of the whore's pillows under my head, "I'd take care of anything with a cock that big. But he's still only a goddamn horse."

Whispered snorts from Ulysses.

116

"You look real natural laid out back there," Doc Peirce said with a note of professionalism. "Nice suit. That's the one Bill Hickok gave me to bury you in. If need be. I really had a busy night after the shoot-out. Got a carpenter to build a coffin. Real nice box, extra long to accommodate you. And had a nice plot to plant you in at Ingleside, a romantic spot on the mountain slope," he paused and shook his head. "A lot of work for naught."

He made me feel like a slacker.

"Henry Stanley wrote a fine account of you. It was in the Deadwood Gulch Gazette," Doc Peirce said and shoved a copy of that newspaper in my hands. "He was a little peeved. The Gazette stole his story from the telegram he sent back East. What did he expect? Newspapers are always stealing from each other. He said he was going to sue them. But I don't see how; he's on his way to Africa."

I quickly looked over the story, which took most of the front page. That is, the space between the advertisements. There was my name. The great journalist had me graduating from the wrong college but what the hell he at least spelled my name right. This was a real thrill. The only thing a correspondent likes to see more than his name over a story is his name in someone else's story.

The crowd cheered as Colonel Cody and Martha Jane mounted the front of the coach. Colonel Cody stood on the seat and waved his Stetson.

"People of Deadwood and the Black Hills, I salute you. I reluctantly have to part now but we will be together again. And sooner than you think. Mister Langrishe and I have struck a deal. I will be the premier attraction at the opening of his new theatre. Following in the tradition of General Custer, I will relate the historical significance of my life. I will tell you the truth of my exploits on the Plains and the real truth of my victory over Yellow Hand and the rest of the Cheyenne. Mister Langrishe will be selling advance tickets on this limited engagement performance, which I assure you will be a sell-out. To make certain of…"

"Bill you have to leave now," the marshal again urged. "The Fifth is almost in town. Listen to the band."

"Yes, yes, good people, I will have to leave you now. But don't forget, walk or run to the Langrishe's box office and purchase your advance tickets if you…"

Apparently Ulysses heeded the urgency more than Colonel Cody did. He started off without a command.

Cheers from the people of Deadwood until we reached the end of Main Street. Garryowen at first increase in volume than grew fainter and fainter as we got further and further from Deadwood.

Colonel Cody and Martha Jane engaged in a lively conversation. Mostly Colonel Cody complaining about Louisa and her lack of affection and Martha Jane complaining how hard it was to find a good man in a saloon and the lack of affection shown towards her.

"You're so quiet, Francis Scott," Martha Jane said. "I hope you're still alive." This evoked har-hars from both of them.

"You look real comfortable back there, Son," Colonel Cody said with undisguised envy. "I could use a little sleep myself. I've been on a long campaign and would have been back in North Platt if Bill Hickok didn't ask me to look after you."

"It does look inviting back there," Martha Jane said. ""I haven't had much sleep these past couple of days taking care of Francis Scott. Not that I'm complaining."

"Why don't the two of you rest up," I said. "I'll do the driving." I made my way forward, grabbing one of the sacks of food on the way.

Faint protests were murmured from the front.

"No, don't worry. I can handle it. Watch. Ulysses! Stop." He did just that and looked back at me. "I want you to go along Strawberry Ridge to Mount Rushmore. When you get hungry or thirsty stop."

He nodded his head, I swear, and started walking again.

"I'll be goddamned," Colonel Cody said as he and Martha Jane crawled in the back and I took the seat up front. "You really have that horse trained. Do you want to sell him?"

I really didn't have to train Ulysses. This was the route Mister Langrishe used and Mount Rushmore was the first stop. And when he got hungry or thirsty he always stopped and let you know about it. Colonel Cody's showmanship was already beginning to rub off on me.

"My God, this is comfortable and cozy," Colonel Cody said. "How about a little afternoon delight, Jane?"

Giggles and shrills from Martha Jane. The coach began to rock and roll. "Not now, Bill." she whispered. Her whispers could be heard halfway across the Black Hills.

"What's wrong? Do you think whats-his-name can hear us," Colonel Cody whispered back. His whispers could probably be heard in War Bonnet Creek. "Look he's all leaned over. He's asleep. Good thing the horse knows the way."

True I was leaned over. But I was far from asleep. The excitement of this past summer, my summer with Mister Hickok and Kit, was in my thoughts and spinning around. Would there ever be another summer like this? Would Deadwood ever be as exciting again? Would my life ever be the same? Before I had too much time to dwell on these ponderous thoughts, Martha Jane shrilled me out of my reverie.

"No. Not until you tell me where Bill Cody and George are."

"I can't tell you, Jane, I have a sacred trust."

"Bunk. If you want to thrust anything into this pussy, you better tell me. Besides, I can be trusted and should know where they are in case something happens to you."

"You make a good argument, Jane. You sure that boy's asleep?" Colonel Cody asked and paused. "I don't know why he wants to go back East. I can use someone like him for my Wild West Show. A writer familiar with newspapers. He can be my agent to deal with the press. I can use his horse too."

"We'll talk about that later. Tell me where they're at."

"They're on their way to Michigan."

"Michigan? The family homestead in Monroe?"

"No. That would be too reckless. But it isn't far from there. Near Detroit. They'd be able to cross over to Canada if they needed to. Detroit is becoming quite an industrial city. They might try to contact some manufacturers to sell their tin. They might stay there a couple of weeks, a month. Hard telling. After that they want to search for Crazy Horse. George thinks he can clear his name if he gets Crazy Horse to testify. We all figure the

119

Deadwood shoot-out will clear itself as soon as General Merritt concludes his investigation."

"Bill, slow down and just tell me where this place is. Is there an address of someone to be contacted?"

"They'll be at a farm in a little village called Dearborn. That's where George holed up after the Army ordered his arrest. It was close enough so Libbie could sneak in at nights."

"Bill Cody. Don't be so goddamn exasperating. Whose farm is it?"

"It's owned by a William…but wait. Don't use his name. He's too well known in Dearborn and could get in trouble. George said to contact his son. He'll get the message to his father. He's a young fella, about thirteen."

"Thirteen?"

"Don't be taken back by his age. When I was thirteen I was already riding for the Pony Express…"

I almost jumped out of the coach.

"…But don't worry, Jane. He's the cleverest boy you'll ever meet. He's already a crackajack. He repaired my watch when I visited George there."

"What's his name?"

"Henry. Henry Ford."

-The End-

About the Author

Len Wildes is an Air Force veteran, graduate of Penn State University and a survivor of many years in journalism. He is interested in everything and has a century of unfinished projects to complete. But in the meantime he seeks the truth, whatever that may be.